Shropshire Walks
with
Ghosts and Legends

Dorothy Nicolle

Published by Sigma Leisure – an imprint of
Sigma Press, 5 Alton Road, Wilmslow, Cheshire SK9 5DY, England.

British Library Cataloguing in Publication Data
A CIP record for this book is available from the British Library.

ISBN: 1-85058-791-4

Typesetting and Design by: Sigma Press, Wilmslow, Cheshire.

Cover photographs: clockwise from top left – Shrewsbury Castle (Walk 7), Pontesford Hill (Walk 9), the bridge at Ironbridge (Walk 17), the Feathers Hotel at Ludlow (Walk 20). *All photographs by the author.*

Maps: the author; reproduced from Ordnance Survey mapping on behalf of The Controller of Her Majesty's Stationery Office © Crown Copyright. Licence Number MC 100032058.

Printed by: Ashford Colour Press Ltd

Disclaimer: the information in this book is given in good faith and is believed to be correct at the time of publication. No responsibility is accepted by either the author or publisher for errors or omissions, or for any loss or injury howsoever caused. Only you can judge your own fitness, competence and experience. Do not rely solely on sketch maps for navigation: we strongly recommend the use of appropriate Ordnance Survey (or equivalent) maps.

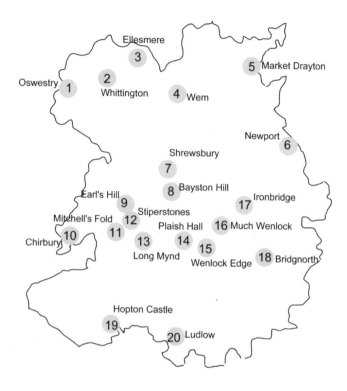

Ellesmere
3

Oswestry
1
2
Whittington
4 Wem

5 Market Drayton

Newport
6

Shrewsbury
7

8 Bayston Hill

Earl's Hill
9
Stiperstones
Mitchell's Fold
12
Ironbridge
17

11
Plaish Hall
16 Much Wenlock

Chirbury
10
13
14
15

Long Mynd
Wenlock Edge
18 Bridgnorth

Hopton Castle
19

20 Ludlow

Key to Maps

· · · · · · · · Route of walk   ‿‿ Bridge   Deciduous or mixed forest   Castle

——— Road   +++++ Railway   Conifer plantation   Church

········· Track   ← UP DN → Steep slope   Marsh

Contents

Introduction

Shropshire is a stunningly beautiful county. The local people say that when God made Paradise he was only practising. Having studied all the imperfections that were to be found in Paradise, he then made Perfection – Shropshire.

Indeed, when I first came to live in the county some years ago, an estate agent once described Shropshire to me as 'the county that kills ambition'. By this he meant that people come to live here from other parts of Britain, thinking that they will stay only a few years and then, when an opportunity arises on their career ladders, they plan to move on. But they don't. Instead, when that promotion is offered they decide that the quality of life here is so good that, promotions notwithstanding, they would prefer to stay in Shropshire.

It is not only the living that feel this way about the county. It would appear that the dead do so too. It seems to be that, even when they die, many people do not want to leave. They prefer to keep their ties to the buildings and places that they knew when alive – so that Shropshire is now one of the most haunted counties in England.

In fact, there are at least 500 places in the county that are known to be haunted. And those are only the ghosts that people mention. Who knows how many there are altogether? Indeed, the ghostly tally seems to grow all the time!

And it is not just ghost stories that abound in Shropshire. There are the legends too. Legends everywhere you look. It does not matter where you go in the county. Wherever you are you can look around and see places that are associated either with a ghost story or with a legend. Some of these legends must be truly ancient and it is difficult to see where some of the old stories came from. Some 'legends' are relatively new – can the story of Bridgnorth's cannon be true? Or has some local joker made up a story that has already passed into the local folklore?

The stories abound. For example stand on the top of Grinshill in the north of the county and look at the surrounding countryside. Look east and there's Moreton Corbet Castle, haunted by a man who wants to ensure that the great Tudor mansion is never rebuilt. You can see the Wrekin, said to have been made by a bad-tempered giant.

Or the hill of Nescliffe where Shropshire's Robin Hood had his hide-out.

Similarly, if you should find yourself on a hilltop anywhere in the south of the county, Earl's Hill for example, the same applies. Earl's Hill, just outside Pontesbury, is associated with legends that must date back to Saxon times. Looking east from there your eye first falls on the hills of the Stiperstones, with the Devil's Chair, easily recognisable from its jagged outline. And then there are the hills to the west that form the border between England and Wales where Owen Glendwr is said to still walk.

But why is it that Shropshire, in particular, seems to be especially full of ghost stories and other legends? I think it is easy to understand when you consider where the county is positioned, in the middle of the Welsh Marches, on the border between England and Wales. It's an area where two cultures have met and mingled. The Welsh, the ancient Celts and earliest inhabitants of the area, have a long bardic tradition. Their love of story telling is well known.

Into this area arrived the Anglo-Saxons who brought with them an entirely different tradition for story-telling – just how ancient the story of Beowulf is, is anyone's guess. But they also brought something new. They brought a language that is particularly rich. English is a language that lends itself to story-telling; it's a language that can be played with and, even today, is still constantly being enriched.

So it was here that these two traditions, or cultures, mixed. Is it any wonder that Shropshire has such a wealth of old stories? But that's not the end of it. The tradition for story-telling continues to this day with people meeting once a month in the Wenlock Edge Inn to tell their tales, both ancient and modern. New stories are constantly being added to the local collection.

And where else in the world could you find a museum especially dedicated to myths and legends? Such a museum, if it exists at all, must be in Shropshire. And, sure enough, Mythstories, the world's first story museum, can be found in Wem.

So, go for a walk and enjoy the stories that survive wherever you go! And, if you stop to chat with local people as you walk along, then the chances are that you will go home having heard many new ones!

The walks

The walks in this book are aimed at all those who enjoy a walk and a story, young and old. None of the walks in the book is particularly strenuous. However, there are many that include short, but sometimes quite steep climbs.

Different people walk at different speeds. The times given for the various walks are for adults walking at a steady, but moderate, pace with occasional stops to admire the view. If walking with children you will need to allow more time for the walks

Maps

The maps in the book have been kept very simple but should be easy to follow. However, it is strongly recommended that you also always use the relevant Ordnance Survey Landranger or Explorer Map as well. Occasionally, changes are made on the ground and these more detailed maps will, therefore, sometimes be required.

The Ordnance Survey (OS) maps also give far more detail concerning the general lie of the land regarding, for example, the potential steepness of slopes.

Directions

When you cross a stile take a moment before you climb over to look for the arrow on the stile itself, as these will generally show you the direction in which the walk continues. When reading the direction in the book it is best to stand with your back to the stile before bearing to right or to left.

Footpaths often go directly across a field and, if the field is under crops, it can sometimes be hard to see just where you should go. Look carefully for the stile at the exit of the field and then walk, in single file, in as straight a line as possible, across the field towards the exit. Alternatively, it is sometimes best to walk around the crops. Use common sense when deciding how to go.

Clothing and footwear

It is essential that you wear suitable, stout footwear. It is not advisable to wear trainers, even in summer, for the walks. Many of the walks go through fields with livestock; cows and horses can easily churn up a section of a footpath, forming deep holes in the turf – or other things may make it decidedly unpleasant without suitable boots or shoes!

Even on hot, sunny days, it is generally advisable to wear long trousers when walking through fields and over stiles. The stiles, particularly, soon become overgrown with nettles and thistles.

When walking on the hills it is always advisable to carry windproof or waterproof coats in case the weather should turn nasty.

Dogs

All these walks, apart from the one in Shrewsbury which is entirely within the town, are suitable for well-behaved dogs. However, there are occasions when you need to cross or walk for short distances along busy roads.

Shropshire is a rural county and the walks often go through areas with livestock in the fields or sheep grazing on open hills. Dogs must be kept under close control at all times. Even the best tempered farmer will have good reason to be angry should he see you walk, accompanied by dogs that are not on leads, through a field amongst ewes that are heavily pregnant or with very young lambs. At such times, even the best-behaved animals should be kept on leads.

Many of the stiles that need to be crossed are quite high and dogs will often need help to climb over them. Do not attempt to make holes in the fencing for dogs – small lambs seem to be able to discover any hole in a hedge!

Above all, wherever and whenever you walk remember the main rule of the countryside: **take only photos and leave only footprints.**

Walk 1: Oswestry

Where kings once fought

Distance and time: 7 miles (10.5km); 3.5 hours.

Starting point: Festival Square, Oswestry, beside the statue of the Borderland Farmer. There are numerous car parks nearby – please note that most of these are Pay and Display car parks.

Maps: Landranger Map 126 or Explorer Map 240.

Terrain: Footpaths through fields and country lanes with a steady climb up onto Offa's Dyke in the middle of the walk. There are eight stiles.

Refreshments and toilets: None on the walk itself; numerous pubs and coffee shops in Oswestry.

Useful contacts: Oswestry Tourist Information and Heritage Centre – 01691 662753

Introduction

Oswestry has seen a turbulent past and has changed hands many times as the English/Welsh border has been moved to one side or other of the town. In fact its history of warfare goes back even earlier than the late AD700s when King Offa of Mercia decided that a proper demarcation line should be enforced and ordered that the dyke be built.

The Walk

Festival Square is close to the town centre overlooking Church Street.

1. From the statue of the Borderland Farmer walk left down Church Street towards St Oswald's church, as far as the traffic lights. Cross over the road and walk up Upper Brook Street. At the second road on the right, turn into Oswald Place. This road soon becomes St Oswald's Well Lane.

    Look out for St Oswald's Well on the left-hand side of the road. Oswestry was the site of a great battle that took place in the year

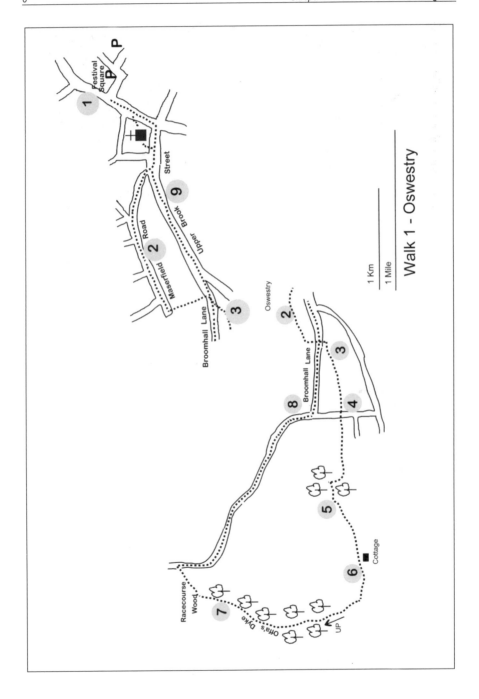

Walk 1 - Oswestry

1 Km

1 Mile

St Oswald's Well

AD642. The battle was fought between the pagan king of Mercia, King Penda (who, incidentally, introduced a safe coinage within his realm and thus gave his name to our "penny") and the Christian king of Northumbria, King Oswald.

During the course of the battle King Oswald was killed. As was the inevitable custom of the time, his body was mutilated after the battle and bits of him were hung up for all to see in a tree on the battlefield site. This is where the town gets its name – Oswestry simply means Oswald's tree!

The old stories tell us that an eagle flew over the battlefield, came down to the tree, picked up one of Oswald's limbs and flew off with it. A short distance away, the eagle dropped the limb and, where it hit the ground, a well miraculously bubbled up.

It must be remembered that King Oswald had been a Christian, killed in battle fighting against a pagan king, and so he was immediately venerated as a saint by Christians all over the country. Many came on pilgrimage to the place where he had died and visited this holy well. Many, also, took away with them a small souvenir of their visit – a cupful of soil from just in front of the well. The Venerable Bede, writing his 'History of the English Church and People' some seventy years later, described how so many people had visited and taken away a cupful of the holy soil that a hollow had been carved out in front of the well. As you will see, the hollow is still there!

2. Continue with the walk by following the road as far as it goes (the road from here is called Maserfield Road – the battle between Penda and Oswald came to be known as the Battle of Maserfield). At the end, turn left along the bridleway and then through a metal gate onto the road beyond, Broomhall Lane. Turn right and, just past the second red brick building on the other side of the road, there is a footpath with a stile into a field.

3. Walk across the field, bearing slightly to the left, and over a second stile. In the second field, a old trackway is clearly defined. Follow this to the far end of the field, which you leave via a third stile.

4. Cross over the tarmac road and enter the next field by climbing over a very high, stepped stile. In this field, there is again a clearly defined gravel track, which you follow to the far end where it turns right and climbs a slight hill. Walk past two concrete gateposts, which seem to stand in the middle of nowhere. Beyond these, there is another gate with a stile beside it, which leads into a wooded area. This can be quite overgrown with nettles in summertime but the path goes through it and then turns left following the outside of a wall of a former large vegetable garden. You emerge from the woodland into an open field that you walk straight across.

5. Cross into another field over a stile. Notice that on this stile there are two arrows pointing diagonally to right and to left. Follow the left-hand arm, which really leads you straight across the field. At the far end of the field, there is a cottage just beyond the right-hand corner – the footpath goes through a gate and behind this cottage.

6. Just behind the cottage outhouses there is a footpath indicated to the right which climbs steeply for about 10 metres before levelling off. This comes on to a gravel track where you go straight on and then, as the track turns sharply left once more, you leave it to walk straight on. There are a number of tracks here – keep walking in a westerly direction until you come to the Offa's Dyke Path. This is clearly marked with a signpost with an

acorn symbol on it. Here you turn right onto the path and start walking steeply uphill.

King Offa was King of Mercia in the 8th century. He was a phenomenally powerful king, a contemporary and rival to Charlemagne. Descended, it is said, from the god, Woden, Offa was the first king to describe himself as the King of all the English, not just King of Mercia.

Today we think of Mercia as an early Midlands region and, indeed, that is all it was when Offa came to the throne. However, by the time he died he had extended his territories to include all of East Anglia and south-eastern England, all the way into present-day Hampshire. London, for example, was therefore firmly within his territory.

Offa ordered that the Dyke should be built to define the western boundary of his kingdom and keep the Welsh (or foreigners) out. Incidentally, the very word "Welsh" comes from a Saxon word that meant "foreigner" – a bit cheeky on the part of the Saxons when you consider that it was the Welsh who were the true natives of Britain and the Saxons who were the new settlers!

The Dyke extends for some 70 miles and was the major building project of its time, the largest Anglo-Saxon earthwork in Europe. Walking along this stretch of the Dyke it is possible to see just what a massive project it was – and this, despite the 1000 years of erosion that has taken place since it was built.

7. You now follow the Offa's Dyke path for just over one mile before emerging from the forest over a stile onto open heath land. Here there is a fork in the paths – take the path to the right which leads eventually to a tarmac country lane where you turn right to walk back down the hill towards Oswestry.

8. This road eventually brings you back to Broomhall Lane where, earlier, you came through the metal gate onto this road. This time you continue straight on down the road which soon comes into Upper Brook Street.

You pass the entrance to Oswestry College which was founded as early as 1407. Across the road, you will see the rugby fields and local tradition has it that it was here that the Battle of Maserfield between Penda and Oswald actually took place. Penda was also to be killed in battle eventually – he was defeated by Oswald's brother some twelve years later.

There is a final postscript to the story of King, or rather Saint, Oswald's limbs. Throughout medieval times, the bones of saints were the most precious of relics and St Oswald's bones were especially prized. Some years before his death Oswald had been dining with St Aiden one Easter when he was told that a crowd of hungry beggars was at the door. He promptly ordered that his own food should be distributed to them. Aiden was so impressed by this gesture that he turned to Oswald, seized his right-hand and said, "May this hand never wither with age". Years after Oswald's death, so it is said, his hand and arm were still in perfect condition preserved in a silver casket in Bamburgh.

Other parts of Oswald's body were used as relics too – he could be said to have travelled further after he was dead that he ever did while alive! His head ended up at Durham Cathedral, along with a bone from one of his arms. A leg bone was later given to the Pope at the Vatican. And two other arm bones were to reach cathedrals as far away as Coblenz and Prague. And those are just the bones we know about!

9.   Walk beyond the school towards the centre of Oswestry but, before you reach the traffic lights, turn to the left along a footpath signposted to the Tourist Information Office and St Oswald's church. The TIC occupies the town's Heritage Centre in a delightful timber-framed building that was the original home for Oswestry College. From the Heritage Centre, walk around the right-hand side of St Oswald's church and onto Church Street where you turn left and walk back to Festival Square.

As you walk past one of the entrances to Oswestry College you may notice the words 'LAST DAY' painted in white on a brick wall. The story is that one schoolboy, on his last day at school painted the words here. It has since become a school tradition that, on the last day of the summer term, one of the final year boys repaints the words. It is in this way that traditions, and legends, begin.

Walk 2: Whittington
Jack the Lad

Distance and time: 8 miles (13km); 4 hours.

Starting point: The car park behind Whittington Castle. Please note that there is an honesty box in the car park for users to make a voluntary payment for parking here.

Maps: Landranger Map 126 or Explorer Map 240.

Terrain: This is a very pleasant walk with no climbs. There are, however, 13 stiles and one gate to be climbed. The whole area was formerly marshland, which was drained in the 17th and 18th centuries, and one section near the beginning can be boggy after sustained rain.

Refreshments and toilets: There are a couple of pubs in Whittington and two further pubs along the course of the walk.

Introduction

It is said that King Arthur once lost his sense of chivalry and came to stay at a chapel locally where he recuperated and found his courage and goodness once again. Local people also would like to believe that Dick Whittington, Lord Mayor of London, came from here but I think that this is unlikely. However, there are many other legends associated with this area instead.

The walk

There was a castle on this site in Saxon times and this early castle is known to have been captured by Roger de Montgomery soon after the Norman conquest of England. However, the present castle, the gatehouse of which survives today, was probably built by Fulke FitzWarin in the early 1200s.

Fulke Fitzwarin and the young Prince John quarrelled as children and had a fight during which the prince was hit on the head. The prince then complained to his father but King Henry refused to punish young Fulke saying, instead, that the fight was probably John's own fault. It was a slight that John never forgave.

Whittington Castle

Fulke's family had owned the castle for some years but it was lost in battle to the Welshman, Moris de Powis, not long before John became King. Remembering his old hatred of Fulke, John refused to help him to regain his lands and so, in response, Fulke refused to serve the new king. He became an outlaw threatening anyone who served John, killing those of the King's knights who came hunting him and stealing from the King's merchants as they went about their lawful business. John became so angry that he promised a reward of £1000 to anyone who could bring him Fulke's head and so Fulke, wisely, escaped to Europe.

If the legends are to be believed, Fulke Fitzwarin had more adventures than would seem to be possible, travelling all around Europe and working as a mercenary soldier for both the King of France and the King of Barbary. He found time, also, to rescue the daughter of the King of Carthage who was being held prisoner by a fierce dragon in his cave, surrounded by all his treasure.

Eventually King John died and Fulke returned to England to once again lay claim to his estates which, this time, were returned to him.

As an old man, however, he worried that he had killed so many people during his lifetime. One night, while thinking of how best to atone for all his sins, a bright light suddenly shone around him and a voice told him to build an abbey as a penance. When the light faded, Fulke found that he could no longer see. He went ahead and did indeed build an abbey – on his lands at Alberbury – but he never regained his sight.

1. Leave the car park by walking towards the church. Turn left up the main road (the B5009) and right into Top Street. Turn left

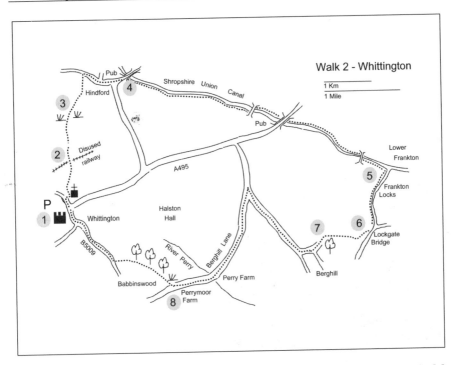

into Daisy Lane, walk to the end of the lane and enter the field beyond, waymarked with a footpath sign. The path leads straight ahead to the far end of the field, over a stile from where the next stile can be seen in the hedge on the left-hand side of the next field. After crossing the second stile, you find yourself beside a disused railway line, which you also cross – the third stile is slightly to your right, behind a crab apple tree.

2. On entering the field bear right, following a clearly defined track – the route is clearly marked with yellow arrows and leads you into another field where you bear left. Take care when following the yellow arrows that you walk in the direction in which they point. Crossing over a stile at the bottom of the field you enter a field covered in reeds which could be a quagmire following wet weather. Leave this field by passing over a wooden footbridge – take care because some of the planks in the bridge are a bit rotten.

The stream that you have just passed over is one of the many drainage channels here. Some 400 years ago all of this land was marsh and agriculturally quite unproductive. Today, after severe rain it can still become very boggy.

3. Walk directly across this field, over another wooden bridge and around the new fencing bearing generally towards the right until you come to a gate leading onto a lane. Follow this until, crossing another stile you find yourself on a tarmac T-junction. Turn to the right and walk into the village of Hindford. In Hindford, follow the road sign to Lower Ridge, passing the Jack Mytton Inn on your left.

Jack Mytton was, without a doubt, one of Shropshire's most colourful characters. He was born in 1796 and inherited an enormous fortune when he was still aged only two. Throughout his childhood, Jack was thoroughly spoilt. He was expelled from both Westminster and Harrow schools and was then educated by a private tutor.

Apparently, the only subject that he thought was of any interest at all was the Greek classics.

Then, as soon as he was old enough to have control of this fortune, he began to work his way through it. Jack was a man who could never refuse a dare. The pub sign here, for example, depicts him riding on the back of a bear as a result of being dared to do so. He was an accomplished huntsman and one story relates how he once released two foxes in the dining room of the Lion Hotel in Shrewsbury and terrified all the other guests as he chased them with his hounds.

The sign for the Jack Mytton Inn

His home was Halston Hall which is in the centre of the route of this walk. An inveterate gambler, Jack eventually was forced to sell the entire contents of the house to attempt to pay his debts and fled the country for a time. However, on his return to England he was arrested for debt and he eventually died, half mad and quoting Sophocles to the end, in a debtors' prison in London, aged only 37.

Jack is buried in the church in the grounds of Halston Hall. But he has not left us altogether. Each year, on his birthday (30 September) he haunts the Mytton and Mermaid pub in Atcham. Apparently, this is because the people bringing his body back from London for burial stopped in Atcham for the last night before his funeral.

4. From the Jack Mytton pub walk towards the canal bridge but, before crossing the bridge, take the path on the left through a gate onto the towpath of the Shropshire Union Canal. Turn to the right so that you are walking with the canal on your left. Follow the towpath for the next 2.5 miles. There are a number of bridges over the canal. On two occasions the towpath changes sides crossing over a bridge. The path is clearly defined in each case. Eventually you reach the hamlet of Lower Frankton where the Shropshire Union Canal meets the Montgomery Canal. Turn right towards Montgomery, walking beside a group of three sets of locks.

5. Follow the Montgomery Canal for about half a mile passing under the Lockgate Bridge. Before reaching the next lock on the canal, turn right onto a footpath.

6. For the next half a mile there are no public footpath signs. However, the start of the path is clearly defined by a red brick bridge with a wooden gate at the end of it. This leads into a field; walk directly across this field and climb over the fence at the far end into another field. In the next field turn slightly towards the left to walk across the field, under the pylons. The exit from the field is through a gate at the far end and this leads onto a well-established track where you turn to the left.

7. Follow the track until it reaches a tarmac country lane and turn right. Keep going right at the next junction and after half a mile

you will reach a T-junction where you turn left towards the village of Babbinswood. Follow the lane for the next mile until, just beyond Perrymoor Farm, the next section of footpath is indicated over a stile on the right.

You are now skirting the village of Babbinswood or, so it is said, Babies' Wood. This is where, according to many local people, the story of the Babes in the Wood really did happen. The fairy story, of course, relates how the two children wandered alone into the forest and got lost. Modern versions of the story usually describe how they became tired and eventually fell asleep under a large tree. Here the gentle creatures of the forest looked after them, covering them with a blanket of leaves and keeping them warm until they were found and taken home to their families and to safety.

It's a sad fact of life that so many of our old fairy stories and legends are based on events that did indeed happen. Undoubtedly the true story here tells of two children who got lost or were abducted and whose bodies were found weeks or even years later, buried under the leaves of the forest. Perhaps such an event happened locally and was remembered simply because the name of the village was deemed to be so apt. In reality the name probably dates from Saxon times and will have had little to do with "babes".

8. The footpath around Babbinswood is clearly defined with yellow arrow waymarkers and crosses over several stiles. Again, take care when following the yellow arrows to walk in the direction indicated in each case. The last stile is the one onto the main road once more, where you turn right and walk back towards Whittington.

As you approach the car park through the castle gatehouse, look carefully at the castle's windows – you might just see the faces of two ghostly children peering out. If you do see them you are looking at the faces of two children who lived here many centuries ago and who continue to haunt the castle.

Walk 3: Ellesmere
How a lake was formed

Distance and time: 7.5 miles (11km); 3 to 4 hours.

Starting point: Car park and picnic area at Castle Field, the entrance to which is opposite the Boat House coffee shop.

Maps: Landranger Map 126 or Explorer Map 241.

Terrain: Some gentle hills but much of the walk is along the flat canal towpath. There are nine stiles.

Refreshments and toilets: None on the route of the walk until you reach the Visitor Centre (with its Heronry) and the Boat House coffee shop at the end, both of which overlook the Mere. There is a pub, the Sun, in the village of Welshampton. There are also many pubs and coffee shops in Ellesmere itself.

Useful contacts: Ellesmere Visitor Centre – 01691 622981

Introduction

Ellesmere is in the heart of what is aptly described as Shropshire's Lake District. The region abounds with numerous small hummocky hills, which are the result of mounds of moraine being dumped by receding glaciers at the end of the last Ice Age. As this earth was dumped, large areas of water were left trapped amongst the small hills that had been formed. Many of these lakes have long since dried out but some were so big that they survive to this day as quite substantial meres.

The Walk

The walk starts from the car park which is on the south-western side of the A528 as it passes just to the south of the Mere. The entrance is just beside the pedestrian crossing opposite the Boat House coffee shop. There is a Pay and Display charge in the car park.

1. Start the walk by leaving the car park at the end furthest from the entrance – there is a footpath here that leads through a kissing

The Shropshire Union Canal

gate, across the tarmac road of Sandy Lane and through a second kissing gate into a Shropshire Wildlife Trust Nature Reserve. Follow the footpath signs to the Canal Towpath, at this point the arrows to follow are painted green.

2. On reaching the canal turn to the left and follow the towpath for the next 3 miles. The route is along the left-hand side of the canal and goes under the Ellesmere Tunnel and then the next six bridges.

3. Each bridge has a numbered plaque on the far side. After passing under bridge number 51 leave the towpath and turn to your right on the tarmac lane, northwards to the village of Welshampton. Walk through the village and turn left beside the church onto the A495. Cross over the road, walking towards Ellesmere, past the village school almost to the end of the village.

4. Just as you are about to leave the village there is a red brick farm-house on the right with a footpath sign leading through its farm-yard. At the far end of this, there is gravel track with yellow

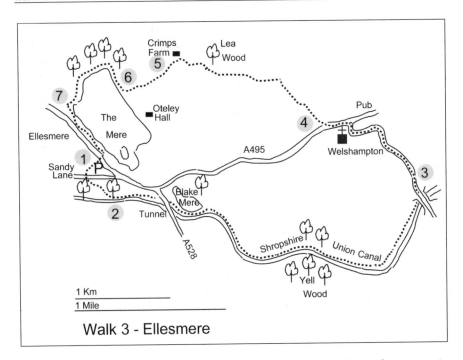

Walk 3 - Ellesmere

arrow waymarkers indicating the route. From here the route is clearly marked through several fields with each gate or stile having a yellow arrow on it, finishing as a trackway leading to Crimps Farm just over one mile away.

Ahead you will see Oteley Hall — a conglomeration today of the hall itself and numerous farm buildings. There have been houses on this site for many centuries but the present building was built as recently as 1963.

However, when you knock an old house down it doesn't do to disturb the resident ghost, in this case a White Lady. Consequently, when the new house was built an old chimney from the earlier building was incorporated into the new structure in order, hopefully, to appease the ghost.

5. Just as the track turns to the right into the farmyard at Crimps Farm there is a footpath sign directing you into a field ahead where you bear left. Again, the route is clearly indicated all the way by the yellow arrow markers.

6. Just before you reach the edge of the Mere there is a footpath sign pointing into the woodland on the right over a stile. A further two stiles have to be crossed and you will find yourself on the well-worn track around the Mere. Follow this to the entrance of the park.

    The topography of this region is well known as being the result of the effects of the last Ice Age. However, local legend has it that Ellesmere's Mere was formed in another way altogether.

    Once upon a time there was an old lady who lived somewhere here. She had a well in her garden that supplied the most wonderful fresh water. One day the old lady's neighbour came to her saying that the neighbouring well had dried up and asking if she could have some water from the old lady's well.

    "No, you can't", said the old lady, who wasn't a very friendly old lady at all, "Go away!"

    The spirit of the well heard the old lady refusing to share her water and was quite horrified. So the spirit decided to teach her a lesson. It made the water bubble up out of the well so that there was plenty of water for all the neighbours. But the spirit wasn't satisfied with just supplying water for everyone. Instead, it ensured that the water continued to bubble up until the old lady, her well and all of her garden was covered with water, never to be seen again. And so The Mere was formed.

7. On reaching the road, continue along the side of the Mere back to the pedestrian crossing, where you can cross over before going through the kissing gate on the other side and up the slope back to the car park.

    If you should stop at the Heronry to watch the birds you may notice a small island where many of them nest. It's not natural. Some years ago, members of the family at Oteley Hall were doing some work in their gardens and had enormous amounts of earth to get rid of. It was a cold winter and the lake was totally frozen over. So they dumped their spoil on the ice. When the spring came the ice melted and this island was formed.

Walk 4: Wem
A newly discovered ghost

Distance and time: 5.5 miles (9km); 3 hours.

Starting point: Park in the station car park in Wem.

Maps: Landranger Map 126 or Explorer Map 241.

Terrain: Easy walking. There is a slight rise at the beginning of the walk to the top of Grinshill. Afterwards the walk descends through agricultural country – this is one of those rarities in country walks, a walk without a single stile all along its route.

Refreshments and toilets: You will pass by two pubs in the course of the walk – the Railway Inn close to the station in Yorton and the Raven in Tilley. There are also many pubs and coffee shops in Wem.

Please note that this is not a circular walk but includes a rail journey. The walk itself starts from Yorton station – this is a *request* stop so please ensure when you buy your ticket from the conductor on board that you mention that you wish to stop at Yorton.

Useful contacts: Mythstories Museum – 01939 235500 (Also, look up the Mythstories website on www.mythstories.com,)

Introduction

Mythstories is a museum of myth and legend promoting a love of literature and writing, poetry and performance but, above all, of stories and storytelling. The museum also arranges story walks during the day, and regular evening story sessions in towns up and down Shropshire, as well as further afield. The Museum is open from April until October although story telling sessions can be arranged for groups at any time of the year.

The walk

The walk starts from the station car park in Yorton. If you have parked your car in Wem and come on the train from the north you will leave the platform and reach the car park directly. If, however, you have come on the train from the south you will need to leave the station and bear right, under the railway bridge, to come to the start of the walk.

1.   As you come out of the station car park turn right and walk along the tarmac road. Walk past the house on the left-hand side of the road beyond which is a field with an unusually long metal gate. Beside the gate is the first footpath sign. Walk across the field following the direction of the sign and into a second field. Walking in the same direction (you are heading towards the church steeple in the distance) stay in the second field, keeping the hedge line on your left until, at the far end, you reach two gates. The smaller gate, on the left, has a yellow waymarker arrow on it and directs you along a small lane.

2.   When the lane reaches the tarmac road, turn to the right. Walk past Clive Village Club and follow the road as it curves to the left and then meets another road at a T-junction. You have been walking along the Marches Way and, at this point, the route for the Marches Way goes along a lane that you will see directly ahead. Ignore this route but instead enter the church yard by the small metal gate and walk up to the church.

If, like me, you are amused by curious graves take time to look for the "Leap Year" grave. It is the grave of Thomas Green, "late of Shrewsbury" who lies buried just to the south of the church, close to the path. Notice that he died on the 29 February,

Headstone of the Leap Year grave

1835 – that can't be so! Think about it...

3.   Leave the churchyard through the lych gate to the north of the church, and immediately on your right you will see a path that

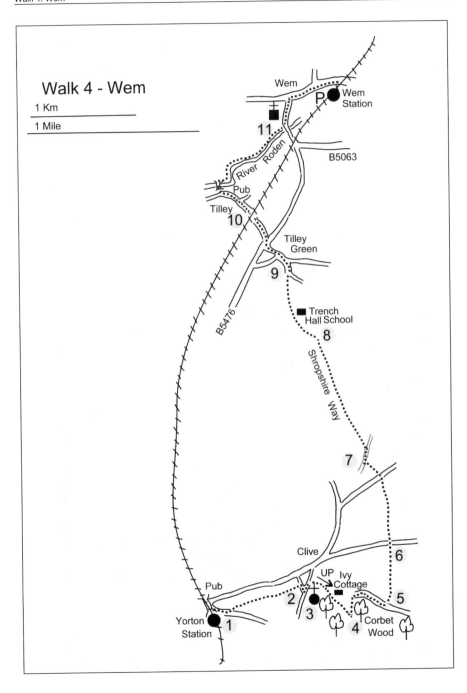

Walk 4 - Wem

1 Km

1 Mile

Wem

P Wem Station

11

B5063

River Roden

Pub

Tilley

10

Tilley Green

9

Trench Hall School

8

B5476

Shropshire Way

7

Clive

6

UP Ivy Cottage

Pub

2

3

5

Yorton Station

1

4

Corbet Wood

leads up the hill. Follow this path, which becomes a wide track, walking past the village's primary school and some houses at the top. Just beyond Ivy Cottage on your left, you will see a white sign, which announces that "The Hardwicke Estate and Clive Parish Council hope you will enjoy your visit to the hill". Follow the path just to the right of this sign that climbs up to the top of The Cliff where you will find a superb panoramic view in all directions.

There is a trig point and a toposcope at the top. The toposcope tells you that you are 630 ft above sea level – no metric measurements here as it was erected in 1977 to commemorate the Queen's Silver Jubilee. For those of you who want to know the metric height, you are 192m above sea level.

Stand by the toposcope and admire the view all around you. Towards the south is Shrewsbury, which is identifiable from its church spires. Beyond Shrewsbury, you will see the hill of Caer Caradoc where the local legends say that the Celtic chieftain, Caractacus, was defeated by the Roman army. Just to the right is the low, flat hill of Long Mynd and then, to the right of that, the Stiperstones with the jagged outcrop of the Devil's Chair on the top.

Turning in a clockwise direction from there you will see the hills of Nesscliffe where the highwayman, Humphrey Kynaston, had his hideout. He is known as Shropshire's Robin Hood so he must have, on one occasion at least, served a good deed to someone. He became an outlaw after killing someone in Church Stretton and was then forced to hide out in a cave in Nesscliffe with his horse, Beelzebub.

Beyond Nesscliffe can be seen the Breidden Hills where, some say, the battle between Caractacus and the Romans was really fought. Turning right you are looking towards the hills of Wales and, continuing to turn clockwise, the lowlands of the Cheshire Plain – the direction in which you will shortly be continuing your walk.

But still admiring the view and turning towards the north-east it used to be said that from here you could see Jodrell Bank. This was certainly possible, on exceptionally clear days, but would be difficult now as the trees have grown too tall. However, closer to hand and still moving in a clockwise direction you will see Hawkstone Hill, identifiable with its tall column rising above the trees. Standing on the top of this column is the statue of Sir Rowland Hill, England's first Protestant Lord Mayor of London who came from Shropshire and, having made his fortune in London, then bought the estate here.

Continuing to turn clockwise you will see the hangars and buildings of the RAF base at Shawbury and perhaps you might be able to make out, beyond them, the ruins of the castle at Moreton Corbet. Although dating from medieval times this castle was extended and turned into a magnificent house towards the end of the 16th century. But today it's a ruin, burnt down during the Civil War and never rebuilt because the site is haunted to ensure that the Corbet family can never rebuild.

The man who haunts the site was called Paul Holmyard and he was a zealous and fanatical Puritan. Arriving at the house one day, he was given shelter and then began preaching to the household in an attempt to convert everyone, from the Corbets themselves down to the youngest scullery maid, to his own particular, fiery brand of Puritanism. In so doing, he upset so many members of the family and their servants that, eventually, driven to distraction by his preaching, the Corbets threw him out. In what would appear to have been a very Christian response (!) Paul Holmyard cursed the entire household saying that they would not have their beautiful new house for much longer. And, sure enough, the house was destroyed by Parliamentary forces in 1644.

Finally, as you continue the clockwise view, you will see the hills of Haughmond from where, it is reputed, Henry IV's queen, Eleanor, watched the Battle of Shrewsbury in 1403. But Henry IV was married twice and neither queen was called Eleanor – so who was Eleanor and what battle was it that she watched from there?

4.   To continue with the walk, turn towards the path that you came along when you climbed up the hill but, instead of returning by the same route, take the next one to the right of it – just on the other side of a buried water tank. Keep to the main path through the bracken, bearing left – do not use any paths that take you to the right – and you will eventually find yourself back on the track that you were on when you came up from the church. Turn to the right and continue along this track.

5.   When you reach a group of three houses (two on the left and one

on the right) you will see, just before the last house, a signpost for the Shropshire Way directing you to the left. You will be now following the Shropshire Way for over two miles. Go through the kissing gate just beyond and walk down the length of the field. Just before you reach the end of the field there is a gate on your right taking you into another field where you continue walking downhill to emerge, through another gate, onto the road just by Clive village.

Walking down this hillside you get clear views of the Berwyn Hills of Wales to the west. It is in these hills that the Welsh patriot, Owen Glendwr, walks to this day. He lived at the turn of the 14th and 15th centuries and was a constant thorn in the sides of the English. However, no-one knows for sure how he died. He just seems to have disappeared from history and so, not surprisingly, it is said that he still walks through the hills of his homeland awaiting the day when he will lead the Welsh to freedom once again.

6. As you come onto the road, follow the Shropshire Way signs which direct you to turn right and then almost immediately left into the field on the other side of the road. The path leads you down the right-hand side of this field, over a small wooden bridge and through two more fields where it emerges onto a gravel track. Cross over the gravel track and follow the signs which direct you along the side of another field and through yet more kissing gates to emerge onto a second trackway – this one no longer in regular use.

7. Note that when you reach the second track the Shropshire Way sign indicates that you should go straight on across the track. However, yellow arrows on the signpost indicate that you should turn to the right – follow the yellow arrows and walk along the track for about 200 metres looking out for a further kissing gate leading into a field on your left. The path from here continues straight ahead, down first the left-hand side of two fields and then down the right-hand side of a field, passing through three further kissing gates on the way. Do not be confused by the field boundaries on the Explorer map – these are incorrect as a number of hedges have obviously been removed.

8. After the last of these kissing gates you will see ahead of you a large building which is a private school. The route takes you to the left of the school grounds, directly across a field in front of the school and through three more kissing gates to come out on a tarmac lane on the other side of the school.

9. At this point you leave the Shropshire Way (which continues on the other side of the lane) and turn to the left to walk down the lane through the hamlet of Tilley Green. At the first road junction bear left, and at the second road junction bear to the right. This takes you to the main road (the B5476) just opposite another lane with, in the middle, a small tree surrounded by a circular metal seat. It was erected to commemorate the coronation of King Edward VII in 1902. Walk up the lane beyond, and over the railway line between two gates.

    Take great care when crossing the railway line. The track bends so that the noise of oncoming trains is not apparent until the trains are almost upon you.

10. Walk through the village of Tilley, bearing left at the first junction and walking past the Raven pub. Just as you come to the other side of the village, beyond a metal garden bench by the roadside, you will see a sign directing you along a footpath beside a field on the right. Follow this path through two kissing gates and over the small bridge ahead of you. Turn right and follow the River Roden downstream, first along the path and then along a gravel track, all the way into Wem.

11. When you reach the main road opposite the old mill, turn left to walk into the centre of town, through the churchyard and then turn right along the High Street. This road will take you, after about half a mile back to the railway station and its adjoining car park, passing the Mythstories Museum on the way.

    As you walk through Wem you will pass, on the left-hand side, the newly rebuilt Town Hall. It was destroyed in a fire in November 1995 when, amongst the spectators watching the fire, one man took a photograph of a ghost that would appear to haunt the building. The ghost was that of a young girl of fourteen, Jane Churm.

Jane Churm lived in 1677 in what is now known as Chapel Street, just opposite the Town Hall. One day she went up to the attic of the house in which she lived, using a candle to see in the darkness. Unfortunately, the roof of the building was made of thatch and the flame from her candle set fire to the thatch. Within minutes, the entire building was ablaze. The fire spread rapidly and much of the town was destroyed as a result. Financially the town of Wem was ruined and it was years and years before it began to recover.

One person was killed in the fire – a shoemaker named Richard Sherratt. Jane, however, survived, grew up and died many years later in Northamptonshire.

Why Jane should haunt the Town Hall rather than the house in which the fire started is an unanswered question. Perhaps it was because this fire broke out so close to where the earlier one had started, that her ghost was attracted to the site.

These days her ghost is said to often appear in the hall in the form of a cold chill that moves around the hall in the evening, usually at around 9.30pm. One evening, however, there was a story-telling session in the Town Hall that had been arranged by the nearby Mythstories museum. Everyone hoped that Jane would manifest herself at the normal time … but nothing happened. But then, when the storytellers had just finished, there was a strange draught that went circling around the room, moving curtains and even the coats on the backs of people's chairs as it went. Jane had obviously enjoyed the stories too much to want to interrupt at her usual time!

There's another strange thing associated with the Town Hall fire. Within the building there was a plaque that commemorated the earlier fire of 1677. When the fire of 1995 occurred this plaque was in the only part of the building that escaped damage. It needed to be restored and cleaned, however, and so it was taken down – and while being removed it was dropped and badly bruised one man's left foot. It was taken to the restorer's workshop and there was another fire while it was there – the plaque was the only thing that was recovered afterwards. It was restored and then brought back to Wem. But on the way back the truck in which it was being transported caught fire – fortunately the plaque wasn't damaged. It was then moved into position once more – and, again it was dropped. It landed on the same man's left foot – but this time it broke a bone. That plaque obviously didn't like being moved.

The Mythstories Museum

Just beyond the Town Hall you will see a sweet shop called The Treacle Mine that recalls a local legend. However, everyone you ask in the town has a different explanation as to what the original treacle mine was and why it existed.

The probable explanation is, on the face of it, quite mundane. From late medieval times, there were two important industries in Wem – tanning and brewing. The by-products from both of these industries drained into the common sewer between them and a strong-smelling sticky, gooey, malty mess it must have been. One man thought he could find a use for it and collected much of the "treacle" and stored it in barrels in his cellar. Some years later a chemist who occupied the building found the barrels and decided to sell it to his customers as a cure-all tonic.

It must have worked, lots of people came back for more. And those who died ... well, as Wem people say "they just went down the treacle mines and never came back".

Walk 5: Market Drayton
The gingerbread town

Distance and time: 9 miles or 5.5 miles (15km or 9km); 3.5 hours or 2.5 hours.

Starting point: Car park beside Queen Street.

Maps: Landranger Map 127 or Explorer Map 243.

Terrain: This is a relatively easy walk, with most of it along quiet country lanes or by the canal towpath. There are seven stiles, all of which are on the longer, extended part of the walk.

Refreshments and toilets: These can be found in Market Drayton. The route of the walk passes the Four Alls pub and tea-rooms at Betton Mill.

Introduction

For many people Market Drayton is synonymous with gingerbread. This seems a strange connection, but it probably comes about because of the town's links with Clive of India who, on his return from the east, brought back with him a taste for spicy foods that continues in this country to this day. The most famous local producer of gingerbread was Billington's, producing gingerbread for customers all over the world since 1817. The exact recipe was a closely guarded secret, handed down from one generation to the next on a strictly "need to know" basis only. Incidentally, if you want to try some gingerbread the correct way to eat it is to cut it into slices and dunk it in port.

The walk

The walk starts from the car park off Queen Street.

1. From the entrance to the car park, turn left and walk down Queen Street; this section of the street is pedestrianised and leads onto High Street where you continue straight on.

    Notice the Corbett Arms Hotel on your left. This is an old coaching inn and many visitors will have passed through its doors over the years. One such visitor came to stay at the hotel in the 1800s. He was very handsome and the chambermaid promptly fell in love with him. Realising her interest, the visitor easily seduced the chambermaid and, when he promised to marry her, she was persuaded that there would be no harm in sleeping with him before they were wed.

One morning, however, she woke up to discover that her lover had left the hotel, leaving no forwarding address. The chambermaid was so ashamed at the way in which she had been led astray that she committed suicide in the room by hanging herself from a hook in the beam in the ceiling. She has haunted room number seven ever since. She still appears, however, but only when a bachelor stays in the room. On these occasions, she will be seen standing at the bottom of the bed and sometimes she will strip the quilt away from it. Occasionally she has even been known to pinch the bottom of any young man who stays there whom she especially fancies.

The chambermaid would also appear to be somewhat light fingered. From time to time items of jewellery go missing in the hotel, only to reappear days, weeks or even months later in the most obvious of places that have been checked many times before. As a visitor staying at the hotel I'm not very sure I could be placated, if any jewellery of mine went missing while I was there, by someone telling me that the ghost must have taken it and it will turn up again in due course!

2.   **Walk beyond the hotel and turn right into Church Street.**

As you walk past the church look up at the tower and try to imagine a seven-year-old boy sitting astride one of the gargoyles at the top. The boy was called Robert Clive and he climbed out onto his perch here some time in the 1730s. He had with him a gazunder – a pot that would "go under" the bed in those days when houses didn't have modern bathrooms! Today we often use the prettier gazunders as ornamental bowls for our pot plants. Robert's gazunder, however, was filled with the contents that they were intended for and he then used this as ammunition with which to pelt the local people as they came to attend a church service.

There are dozens of stories about the terrible things that Robert Clive, the future conqueror of India, did when he was a child. Indeed, he can't have been the best behaved of children as he was expelled from three different schools. Most of the stories, however, weren't told and retold until some years afterwards and so it's difficult for us today to know just how much truth there is in them. But, just like all our legends, there is bound to be an element of truth in them somewhere.

Another story about Robert relates how, in his teens, he ran a gang of hooligans. (It might be said by some that this proved to be excellent training for his future success as a soldier!) His gang would go around the town demanding protection money from the local shopkeepers if they wanted to keep their glass windows from accidentally being broken. One butcher refused to pay, so Robert and his fellow hooligans dammed up a stream that used to run through the centre of the town so that the water (which would have been quite foul) was diverted and flooded the butcher's shop.

3. Walk along the length of Church Street and then turn left into Mount Lane. At the end of Mount Lane, there is a flight of steps leading down the hill. The sign here warns you of "Uneven steps" and they are certainly very uneven and likely to be slippery in wet weather. You can either walk down the steps or, if you prefer, turn right and walk along Love Lane. At the bottom of the steps turn right on Newtown and follow the road as it bears right into Walkmill Road. At this point Love Lane also joins the route once more.

4. Walk along Walkmill Lane and then turn first left onto Sutton Road. The road is unnamed but has a signpost on it directing you to the Market Drayton Golf Course. Cross over the bridge and then follow the road as it bears right all the way to the golf course entrance, which is just over three quarters of a mile away.

As you walk along this road look up on your left and you will see Salisbury Hill. Just on the eastern side of Market Drayton lies the site where the Battle of Blore Heath took place in September 1459. This was one of the many battles of the Wars of the Roses between the Yorkists and the Lancastrians. On this occasion, it was the Yorkists who won and Salisbury Hill was later named for the victorious commander who camped somewhere here on the night after the battle.

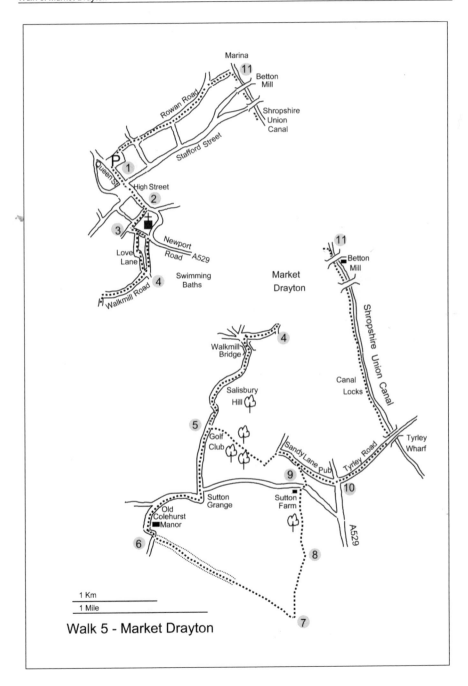

Walk 5 - Market Drayton

5. At the entrance to the golf course the routes diverge. **If you are taking the short walk** the route goes through the club house car park and along the gravel track which you can see ahead of you. This becomes an earthen track; it's a bridleway going up a slight hill. At the top of the rise turn left (the bridleway actually goes to the right at this point). The track then opens onto a tarmac lane, Sandy Lane, where you turn to the right. Follow Sandy Lane as far as the Four Alls pub. The instructions for the route then continue from 'No 10'.

If you are taking the long walk, continue along the tarmac lane for a further mile following the signs for Colehurst and "Old Colehurst 17th C Manor".

As you walk around the house you will catch slight glimpses of a large timber-framed building. This stunningly beautiful house was a dilapidated wreck only a few years ago and has since been lovingly restored. Having been restored it was then opened to the public as a private hotel where, in perfect surroundings, medieval banquets were often held.

There are some ghosts that seem to have an excellent sense of marketing and publicity. I have talked to people who lived here in the earlier years of the 20th century and not one had ever seen nor even sensed a ghostly presence in the building. However, no sooner was the building opened to the public than a handsome young man in 17th-century costume with flowing blond hair was seen walking around the building. This was certainly a description that would fit the owner of the house as well, but there was said to be a ghost of this description too. Not only that, but the owners of the house just happened one day to be visiting an antique shop when, suddenly, they saw an old portrait that looked just like the young man whom they had seen in their house. Naturally, they bought the picture and brought it back.

(As I write this, in the summer of 2002, the house is currently on the market and so its future is uncertain. I wonder if the ghost will stay.)

6. Follow the tarmac road around the house – it first turns sharply left and then turns sharply right. Just as it turns to the right, beside some farm buildings you leave the tarmac road. You will see, just after the road bends, that there is a clearly defined concrete track that leads across the fields just beside, and beyond, the farm buildings. Follow this straight track for the next three quarters of a mile. It leads directly to an old red-brick barn where the track turns sharply to the left. The walk route, however, continues straight on across the field, at the far end of which you will see the first stile. The path leads directly across a second field and stile and then across a third field.

7. At the far end of the third field you will come to another stile but do NOT cross over this one. You will see that there are yellow arrows indicating routes straight ahead and to the left. Follow the arrow that directs you to the left up to the top of the field, where you will see another stile just to the left of a metal gate. Cross over this stile and, taking care to follow the direction of the yellow arrow, walk straight down the length of this field.

8. As you cross over the fourth stile, look back the way you have come and you will get an excellent view of the Wrekin directly to the south of you. In this next field you will see a copse of trees directly ahead of you; bear slightly to the right of it and beyond it, at the far end of the field, you will see a makeshift stile – actually an old metal gate which you climb over. The path follows the left-hand side of the field and comes to another metal gate with a stile beside it beyond which is an overgrown lane used as a dumping area for machinery for Sutton Farm.

9. This overgrown lane opens onto a tarmac country lane where you turn right before, almost immediately, turning left again crossing over your last stile in order to walk down the left-hand side of the field beyond. Walk to the far end of the field and leave the field via a wooden gate beyond which is a very short, overgrown track before you reach Sandy Lane where you turn to the right towards the Four Alls pub.

The name the "Four Alls" can be found in many parts of the country. The sign is at the far side of the pub and shown on it are four people – the King who rules over all, the Bishop who prays for all, the Soldier who fights for all. And then there's you and me – we pay for all! Interestingly, there is an early sign for the pub that hangs on a wall indoors – it was found in the loft some years ago.

The Four Alls is haunted by a lady called Alice. She's a former landlady from as recently as the 1950s – some people never know when to retire!

10. Cross over the main road (the A529) in front of the pub and walk down Tyrley Road, which is just opposite, as far as Tyrley Wharf. When you reach the Shropshire Union Canal turn left to walk along the towpath all the way back to Market Drayton, a distance of nearly two miles. You pass under three bridges altogether.

Each bridge is numbered and, as you come to bridge no 62, look out for the World War II pillbox just to the left. It seems somewhat incongruous here now but, of course, the canals were a vitally important means of transporting goods then and needed to be adequately protected.

Walking along this stretch of the canal you soon become aware of the large number of holiday makers and boat people who use it. As you reach bridge no 63 you will see Betton Mill on the other side of the canal which is a relatively new development in an old mill. Here there is a variety of shops including a tea shop and even a place selling second hand books – just what you need before you join the queue of boats waiting to pass through Tyrley Locks!

11. Continuing along the towpath, just beyond bridge no 63 you will see a sign pointing to the left indicating a footpath into the town centre, half a mile away. Follow the signs which take you through residential streets via Balmoral Drive, Rowan Road and into Longlands Lane. At the end of Longlands Lane do **not**, however, follow the blue sign which tells you to go to the left. Instead turn right and after crossing the road on the pedestrian crossing walk ahead down the little alleyway next to Burgage Building which leads directly back to the car park.

Betton Mill

But before you walk down this alley, just glance up to the right along Smithfield Road because it was somewhere up there that two murderers buried their body. The man who was murdered was called James Harrison. Harrison was due to give evidence in court against a man called Ellson who had been accused of sheep stealing. Ellson's mother, Ann Harris, had hired (at a cost of 50 shillings and a pair of shoes!) the two murderers to carry out the murder so that Harrison couldn't testify against her son. Of course, when Harrison failed to turn up in court the charge of sheep stealing against Ellson had to be dropped.

But it turned out that Ellson was a constant thief and so, inevitably, he was again caught stealing some time later – this time he had taken some potatoes and chickens. In return for his freedom, Ellson then betrayed his mother, his father-in-law (who had also been in the plot) and the two murderers and all four were duly tried and convicted. The murderers were hanged in Shrewsbury in 1828 in front of a crowd of 5000 people. Ellson's mother and father-in-law were also convicted to be hanged but their sentences were later commuted and they were, instead, transported to Botany Bay.

Walk 6: Newport
A plot for Dickens

Distance and time: 6 miles (9km); 2.5 hours.

Starting point: Car park in Water Lane, Newport, overlooking canal.

Maps: Landranger Map 127 or Explorer Maps 242 and 243.

Terrain: A relatively easy walk along well-defined tracks and paths. There are five stiles. The route goes along the verge of the B5062 for a short distance.

Refreshments and toilets: Plenty in Newport. Also there are two pubs in Edgmond, although the route of the walk does not go directly past them.

Introduction

So many of our legends must have developed from events that really happened. These stories were then twisted slightly and embellished so that, years later, it becomes impossible to tell fact from fiction. All fiction writers use real events as the basis for their stories and sometimes it's the genuine stories that seem totally implausible. Could there really have once been someone quite as crazy as Miss Havisham? Oh, yes, and she lived in Newport.

The Walk

Park in the car park opposite Cosy Hall. This is only a small area and can be busy. If this is the case, there is an additional car park further along Water Lane.

1. Leave the car park and turn right into Water Lane and walk towards the main road where you turn right again and cross over the bridge over the former canal.

    Look out for a rather fine Georgian house on the other side of the road and set back slightly, just beyond the Bridge Inn. There was once a lady called Elizabeth Parker who lived here. She was engaged to be married but, on the morning of her wedding, just as she was dressing to go to the church, there came a knock on the door. A messenger had arrived to say that her bridegroom had been killed.

Havisham Court

The shocking news made Elizabeth lose her mind. She vowed that her life had ended at that point in time. All the clocks in the house were stopped and she spent the rest of her days (she lived for a further 40 years) in her bedroom and anteroom. She never took off her wedding dress again. In fact she had one shoe on and was about to put on the second when she heard the news and so, for the rest of her life, she just wore that one shoe and its pair was left on the stool beside her chair. Not only that, but she had the windows of her rooms bricked up so that she never saw daylight again but lived instead by candlelight.

If this story sounds familiar, take a look at the name of the house. It is called Havisham Court. Charles Dickens, who visited Newport on several occasions, must have heard the story of Elizabeth Parker and obviously thought it would make an excellent plot for a book. The book, of course, was called Great Expectations and he named the reclusive lady Miss Havisham. Dickens, however, set the story far away from Shropshire, in Kent.

2. Walk beyond Havisham Court and turn left into Green Lane.

This road quickly becomes a gravel track and ends beside some paddocks. The footpath is signposted over a stile, between the paddocks. Follow the footpath and across a second stile to enter a field. Walk directly across the field. Note that there is a busy road and no fencing at the far end of the field so that young children or dogs must be kept under close control. On reaching the main road (the B5062) turn left to walk along the road – there is no pavement but the verge is quite wide although it does narrow considerably as it reaches the brow of the hill.

This is Cheneyhill on the OS maps. However, for a long time it was known to local people as Madam Piggott's Hill because it was haunted by the ghost of Madam Piggott, who carried her baby in her arms and would sit by an old tree here and comb her ghostly child's hair. Occasionally when an unsuspecting horseman rode by she would jump on the horse's back and cling to the rider as he tried in vain to shake her loose. Only when the rider had to cross a stream or river would she let go – you see ghosts cannot cross over water. Today there aren't many horsemen who travel along this stretch of road.

3.   Cross over the road when it is safe to do so and just beyond the entrance to the Newport Showground you will find a sign indicating a bridleway through the trees. The bridleway opens onto a track alongside a field. Follow this track which bears left at the far end of the field and leads to a country lane opposite Rose Villa, a Victorian house with very decorative brickwork, where you turn to the right to the village of Chetwynd.

It was here that Madam Piggott lived before she died. Madam Piggott was pregnant and, when the time came for her to give birth, the doctor realised that her life was at risk and the baby would probably die too. He warned the squire, her husband, that he could save her but not the baby. Mr Piggott, however, was desperate to have a son and heir and replied to the doctor that "the root must be lopped to save the branch". Appalled by his attitude the doctor tried desperately to save both mother and child, but in vain. They both died. Madam Piggott's spirit was so outraged by her husband's callous attitude that it could not rest and has since wandered through the local countryside.

The story doesn't end there – the squire was so ashamed by his

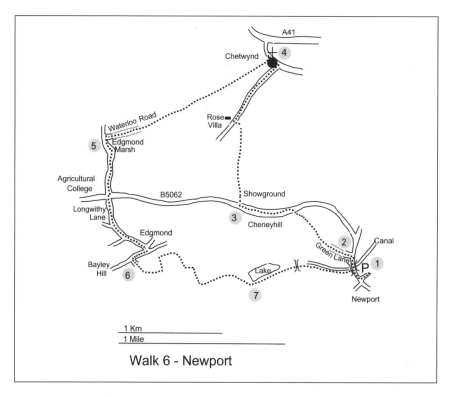

Walk 6 - Newport

action that he couldn't stay in the place where she had died and so moved to live abroad, alone with his guilty conscience.

4. In Chetwynd, walk into the churchyard and out through the lych gate, turning left. The road leads past the Old Schoolhouse (now a private house) beyond which is a footpath into a field on the left. This path goes along the left-hand side of four fields finally emerging over a stile into a gravel track called Waterloo Road, which leads into the small village of Edgmond Marsh.

5. Turn left in Edgmond Marsh onto Marsh Road, cross straight over the B5062, and walk down Longwithy Lane. Follow this road – it changes its name twice, becoming first Pipers Lane and then Stackyard Lane before coming to a road junction where a number of roads meet. Turn right along Bayley Hill (signposted to Lilleshall and Wellington).

6. Just beyond the war memorial turn left down Connors Lane. At the end of this track there is a footpath which leads, over a stile, into a large field. The official footpath goes diagonally across the field to the left. However, the field is obviously used by many local dogwalkers who keep to the edge of the field – do likewise and turn to the left to walk around the field to the far side. Leave the field through a metal kissing gate and follow the well-defined raised path, finally to emerge through another kissing gate before crossing a small concrete bridge over a stream.

St Michael's Church

7. Just over the bridge the path comes to the end of the old canal. From here, you follow the old towpath by the canal all the way back to the car park.

Notice as you pass under the first bridge that there are metal plates attached to the wall. The first one, particularly, is covered in deep grooves. These were caused by the rubbing of the ropes used by the horses to pull the narrow boats along the canal. It does make one wonder how long the ropes themselves lasted!

Walk 7: Shrewsbury

The most haunted town in the country

Distance and time: In terms of mileage, this is the shortest walk in the book. However, in view of the numerous places to stop and explore along the route of this walk, I would suggest that it would be best to expect to spend the best part of a day following this route.

Starting point: Abbey car park, beside Abbey Foregate. Please note that this is a Pay and Display car park.

Map: The Shrewsbury Tourist Information Centre provides free maps of the town for visitors. One of these maps would be ideal to help you follow the route of the walk.

Terrain: This is a town walk along pavements. The climb up Wyle Cop is quite steep.

Refreshments and toilets: Available all along the route of the walk.

Useful contacts: Shrewsbury Tourist Information Centre – 01743 281213

Introduction

That Shrewsbury is an extremely old town there can be no doubt. We will probably never know for sure, but it seems likely that the first people who settled here were Anglo-Saxon invaders, looking for a safe place to make a home. They found it on this hill-top site, almost completely surrounded by the River Severn. It was to prove an excellent choice and, before long, a town was established here that was to grow and become extremely wealthy – we can still see evidence of this wealth in all the marvellous, old timber-framed buildings that survive to this day. Each building exudes history and it is no wonder that many of them have, over the years, come to be associated with the ghosts of past occupants. In fact, Shrewsbury has come to be known as the most haunted town in all of England.

The walk

Start the walk from the car park, opposite Shrewsbury Abbey.

There has been a church on this site since Saxon times. Soon after the Norman Conquest, the old church became an abbey founded in 1083 by Roger de Montgomery, one of William the Conqueror's generals.

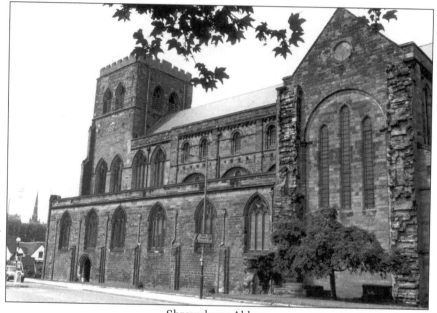

Shrewsbury Abbey

Throughout medieval times Shrewsbury's abbey was the centre for pilgrims wanting to honour St Winifred whose shrine was within. St Winifred, however, had not originated in Shrewsbury. Instead, she was a young girl who had lived in northern Wales in the 7th century. She was a beautiful girl, as they always are in these old legends, and it was therefore inevitable that she should attract the attention of lustful young men. One such, Prince Cradoc, thought he would take advantage of the situation when he found her alone and unattended one day.

Winifred fled from Prince Cradoc towards the village church, but he chased after her and, in his anger, as he caught up with the young girl he drew his sword, swung it at her and sliced her head off.

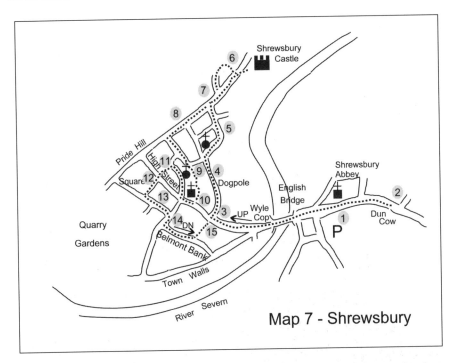

Map 7 - Shrewsbury

Fortunately for Winifred, just as this happened the priest, St Bueno, came out of the church. St Bueno saw what had happened, came up to Winifred, picked her head up off the ground and replaced it on her shoulders. Lo and behold! Winifred came back to life again. Meantime, Prince Cradoc is said to have shrivelled up on the spot, never to be seen again.

Winifred spent the rest of her days in a convent in the hills of Wales. Some four hundred years later, soon after the abbey at Shrewsbury had been established, her remains were brought here so that a magnificent shrine could be built in her honour.

1. Walk from the car park towards the Abbey, but before crossing the road turn to the right to walk up the hill along Abbey Foregate towards the Dun Cow Inn.

All those pilgrims visiting the abbey needed somewhere to stay while they were here and it is therefore likely that the Dun Cow Inn was built for this purpose. As if to prove that it has connections with the abbey, it is haunted by two monks. They can sometimes be seen in the cellar where, presumably, they used to brew ale for thirsty travellers in the past.

But there's another ghost that haunts this building — the ghost of a 17th-century Dutchman who, it would appear, came over to England with King William III, William of Orange. One day, so the story goes, he had an argument with a young squire and killed the boy. He was subsequently brought before the judge, accused and found guilty of the murder, and sentenced to be executed. Apparently he went to his execution complaining bitterly at the unfairness of the sentence — he'd only killed "one Englishman", after all!

2. From the Dun Cow Inn return the way you came, back down along Abbey Foregate and walk past the Abbey, crossing over the road when you have the opportunity. Walk straight ahead to cross over the English Bridge and start climbing up the hill of Wyle Cop.

About half way up the hill you will see the Nag's Head pub on your right which has a most unusual haunting. Look up at the little window on the top floor. Within this room there is a cupboard and within the cupboard there is a painting — and it is actually the painting that is haunted. The painting is of an old prophet and it's said that anyone who looks at it will be driven mad. Certainly, there have been three occasions in the past when people, perfectly sane and seemingly perfectly happy, have stayed in that room and then, for no apparent reason, committed suicide. One was a man who had just been promoted, another was a young girl looking forward to getting married and the third was a First World War soldier who had just returned home from the front. Not surprisingly, the cupboard is always kept locked so that no-one can inadvertently see the painting these days.

The pub has more normal hauntings too. Some work was being done on the building in the early 1980s when a previously unknown panelled room was discovered. Opening the room must have released the ghost associated with it. Perhaps he was also the man in the "funny long coat and hat who came through the wall" that a young girl once saw there.

Before you move on, look across the road at the Lion Hotel. It, too, is haunted, this time by an old lady wearing a Victorian period crinoline who can sometimes be seen walking through a wall near the Adams ballroom in the hotel. Not that she thinks she's walking through a wall – in her day, there was a door at this spot!

3. Continue to walk up Wyle Cop and then turn right into Dogpole. There is no street name at this point but you will almost immediately pass an entrance on your right called Dogpole Court to confirm you are in the correct street. Look for the timber-framed building on the right, sitting back from the road behind an iron fence. This is the Old House and, of course, is haunted.

The Old House has several ghosts, one of which is a man sometimes seen crouching at the top of the stairs who disappears before your eyes. Sometimes the ghost is heard, rather than seen – the sound of his footsteps walking up or down the staircase. This sound is accompanied by the smell of bacon cooking. Or is it the smell of human flesh burning? There is no historical record of any member of the household ever burning to death but it's interesting to note that early owners of the house were Roman Catholics, living at a time of religious persecution in the 16th century. Was a member of the family or someone associated with them perhaps burnt at the stake?

4. Continue to walk along Dogpole. Turn to the right into St Mary's Place, just before you reach St Mary's church and walk toward the Parade Shopping Centre at the far end.

This building used to be the Royal Salop Infirmary and was built in 1830. It ceased to be a hospital in 1977 and has since been converted into flats and shops. Hospitals, sadly, are places where people die and so it is perhaps not surprising that the building is haunted – but not, as it happens, by its patients! In fact, a ghost that was seen on many occasions by members of the nursing staff here came to be known as the "White Lady". She would often be seen beside a patient's bed, looking at the patient lying there. When the nurse on duty saw the White Lady with a patient, she knew immediately that that patient would die during the night.

Another of the ghosts who haunts the old hospital is a former Matron who can sometimes be seen wandering in the area where the operating theatres used to be. And then there's Fred – he haunts the ground floor, close to where the kitchens used to be. It's thought that he was a tramp who would often have turned up here seeking a free meal, something he obviously continues to do to this day!

5. From the front of the old Infirmary turn left to walk along Windsor Place, past St Mary's Waterlane on your right, and out into Castle Street. Here you turn right and walk down to the entrance of Shrewsbury Castle and into the gardens. A wonderful view of the surrounding countryside can be found if you climb the stairs on your right, immediately inside the castle gates, up to Laura's Tower.

What could be more peaceful than the gardens below? Yet, it's this area that is haunted by Bloody Jack. Bloody Jack lived many centuries ago and could best be described as Shrewsbury's Bluebeard. He used to inveigle young girls to the castle with promises of marriage and then have his evil way with them before murdering them. It was the fact that he liked to keep souvenirs of his murders that was to be his undoing. Having killed his victims Bloody Jack would bury the bodies but not before he had cut off the young girls' fingers and toes.

One girl called Mary Ann went missing and her sister, Fanny, came to the castle looking for her. I do feel that these names are bit unlikely but they seem to have entered the local folklore and so we'll stick with them just the same! Fanny made a search for her sister in the castle one day and came across a chest within which she found the evidence of Bloody Jack's crimes — all those dismembered fingers and toes. She rushed into the town to raise the alarm. Jack was then arrested and eventually executed at the top of Wyle Cop where his head was displayed on a pole as a warning to others.

Sometimes Bloody Jack can be seen coming out of the castle and dragging Mary Ann by the hair, across the immaculate lawn in the castle grounds, to her death.

6. Leave the castle and, when you reach Castle Street, cross over the road towards the statue of Charles Darwin in front of the Library, once Shrewsbury School, before turning left to walk along School Gardens.

Sadly for Shrewsbury, Charles Darwin does not haunt his old school. Like most young boys, Darwin is said to have hated his schooldays.

His classmates, incidentally, nicknamed him "Gas" because he was always carrying out experiments in a shed in the garden of the house where he lived in Frankwell, across the river. However, the school is haunted by a lady who, in this case, is known as the "Grey Lady". Who she was no-one knows, so we can only guess that perhaps she was the wife of a former master at the school.

As you walk along School Gardens look out on your right for a courtyard, surrounded by buildings on one of which is the date "1705". These buildings once formed part of the old gaol of the town before the new prison was built at the other side of the castle at the end of the 18th century. One of the offices here has a poltergeist moving things from one place to another. On one occasion a number of people watched, dumbstruck, as a roll of sticky tape apparently seemed to float through the air in front of everyone.

7. School Gardens emerges once again on Castle Street where you turn to the right and walk up the hill to the cross at the top of Pride Hill.

Walking back up along Castle Street towards the centre of the town you pass many buildings with different stories to tell of the ghosts that have been seen. In Castle Court on the right, for example, there are two haunted buildings – one is the old police station haunted by a policeman who once killed himself there and the other is the former Methodist church opposite. There's a man dressed in a blue suit that has occasionally been seen at 15, Castle Street. Even a new shop like Marks and Spencer's would seem to have a ghost – one lady told me once of how she was jostled by someone as she walked down the stairs. But there was nothing there!

One place that should be haunted but isn't, so far as we know, is the area at the top of Pride Hill dominated these days by the cross that was erected in 1952. It was here that, in the past, executions took place. Prince David, the last Welsh Prince of Wales, was executed here in 1283 having been captured in Wales and brought to Shrewsbury to be tried for treason for fighting against the King, Edward I.

Another famous person executed here was Henry Percy, better known as Harry Hotspur. He was very fortunate, actually, because although he was executed after the Battle of Shrewsbury in 1403 he had, in fact, already been dead for some days by then.

There's an interesting story about Hotspur's death. Some years beforehand, when he was still a young man, he had been told by an old witch that he would die near Berwick. Being a Northumberland lad himself, he had automatically assumed that this referred to Berwick on Humber. On the morning of the Battle of Shrewsbury, however, he discovered that the battlefield site was just beside a small hamlet known locally as Berwick. On learning this, his face went white – he knew then that he would meet his death on the battlefield later that day and, indeed, he did.

There may be no ghosts on the actual execution site but ghosts abound in the buildings around. For example upstairs in the branch of WH Smith that overlooks the cross there is the ghost of a woman who, when you see her, appears to disintegrate before your eyes, rather than just simply disappear. Another building near here where a ghost has been seen is, believe it or not, the Burger King outlet on the opposite side of the street – haunted by a soldier in the uniform of the First World War.

8. From the cross at the top of Pride Hill walk down the pedestrian street until, about half way down the street, you see Butcher Row on your left, just before the Thomas Cook travel shop. Turn left into Butcher Row and walk to the far end of the street, beside the entrance to the Prince Rupert Hotel.

If there's a ghost at the Lion Hotel, then surely there must be one at the Prince Rupert Hotel as well and, indeed, there is. In fact, there are two. One of the ghosts is that of a young man who can sometimes be seen in room seven. Staying

The Prince Rupert Hotel

in this room before his wedding day, he was informed that his bride had jilted him and run off with his best man and so he committed suicide here. He often moves things around in the room, which can sometimes be a bit unsettling for visitors who are staying in the room and are unaware that it is haunted.

The other ghost who haunts the Prince Rupert is the ghost of an old man wearing a Victorian nightshirt and nightcap and carrying a candle in his hand. Imagine Ebenezer Scrooge in Charles Dickens' story, 'A Christmas Carol', as he would have appeared on being woken from his sleep by the ghosts of Christmas Past, Present and Future and you probably have a fair impression of just what this ghost looked like. Appropriately enough, he was seen in 1984 by a member of the film crew that was staying here to film 'A Christmas Carol'. Reports of this sighting say that the man who saw the ghost was so frightened by the apparition that he spent the rest of the night in the hotel bar. I wonder if he had already spent quite a bit of time earlier in the evening in the bar too...

9. Walk straight on, past the Prince Rupert Hotel, keeping the church of St Alkmund's on your right. You will find yourself in an open courtyard area with, on the far right-hand side, just outside the churchyard, a small paved passage way. Walk along this, passing an entrance to St Julian's church, until you see a small garden area with an iron gate – this is a former graveyard serving St Julian's church.

Today this is a lovely place to sit and, at lunch time on sunny days many office workers come here to eat their sandwiches and enjoy the peace. It's not always peaceful, however. Sometimes at night terrible groaning noises can be heard coming from the churchyard here. They're the noises made by the ghost of a man who was buried alive some years ago.

This man was a guest at the Lion Hotel in Wyle Cop. He died in his sleep and his body was found the next morning. A search was made through his belongings but there was no sign at all as to who he was, where he came from, where he was going – in fact, nothing that gave any information about the man at all. There was some money, however, and so this was used to pay for his burial in the nearby churchyard of St Julian's.

The next night, terrible moans and groans were heard in the vicinity of the grave and so, the following day his coffin was dug up. When it was opened a terrible sight met everyone. The man was indeed dead by then, but he had obviously woken up at some time and had scratched and clawed at the coffin lid in his attempts to get out.

10. Walk past St Julian's garden and down the steps onto Wyle Cop. Turn right to walk towards the High Street and, just beyond the main entrance to St Julian's church, turn right again into Fish Street and walk up as far as the Three Fishes pub. Above you, you will see the tall spire of St Alkmund's church – it's a bit crowded up there with two people vying to sit at the top.

One of the people who claims this uncomfortable seat is the Devil, himself. He likes to use the spire as a lookout because, from here, he can see all the way to the Stiperstones – and woebetide if he should see anyone sitting in his chair there, because he will then send a storm to wipe them away. In fact, the story of the Devil's association with this spire begins with a terrible storm. It took place in the middle of the 16th century when lightning struck the spire, causing considerable damage, and leaving a mark, said to be that of the Devil's claw, on the church bell.

The other ghost associated with St Alkmund's spire is a ghost with a name – he's called George Archer. He was a steeplejack by trade and so should have known all about the risks involved in climbing up tall spires. However, he got drinking with his mates in the pub just beside you, so the story goes, when one of them made a bet with him that he couldn't climb to the top and turn the weathercock around. Well, of course, George could climb the spire and he immediately began to prove it. He climbed to the top with ease but, full of rum and not a little bravado, when he got to the top he began to wave to all his friends below. He lost his balance and ... whoops ... down he fell. Today he can be seen repeatedly trying to climb to the top to prove his bet and turn that weathercock.

Before you move on look at the delightful timber-framed building ahead of you. It's known as Bear Steps and, as you look at it from here, you will see that there is a shirt shop, inside. This, too, is haunted – by a sad looking gentleman who can occasionally be seen at the rear of the shop.

11. Continue the walk along Fish Street and turn left down Grope Lane, a little alleyway without a name on it, just beyond the Zebra boutique. It is actually a small shut – a 'shut' is a Shropshire term for the narrow, little alleys that could once be found in large numbers, amongst the jumble of buildings in any ancient town such as Shrewsbury.

12. As you emerge from Grope Lane turn right into the High Street and almost immediately you will see, on your left, the open space of The Square. Walk to the far side of the Square, keeping the old Market Hall on your right and then turn left and walk along Princess Street beyond.

    At the far end of the street there is a printing shop on the right – PDC Copyprint. There are a number of ghosts in just this one building. Some very sad ghosts are those of four young children who were trapped in a building that previously stood on this site but was burnt down. Another ghost is thought to be that of their mother, endlessly trying to save them from the fire.

    Another spirit that haunts the building is that of a man who was murdered here. He was stabbed and customers in the building have sometimes felt a sudden pressure in their chests – presumably, the man was killed by being stabbed in his chest. And there's yet another ghost in this building – the ghost, this time, of a young servant girl who was so unhappy for some unknown reason that she hung herself from a beam in one of the rooms. A very sad house, indeed.

13. From Princess Street walk straight on towards the Golden Cross Passage Hotel which you will see on your left with, facing it across the road the remains of Old St Chad's church on the hill opposite.

    Today, it isn't anything like the magnificent church that once used to stand on this site. That church collapsed in 1788 so that only the Lady Chapel remains.

    Some local people insist that this church sits on the site of Pengwern, the legendary palace of the old kings of Powys, established long before the time when the Saxons arrived and founded their town here. However, there are a number of other places that also claim to be the site of Pengwern. Most historians believe that Pengwern would have been either at Baschurch or perhaps Uriconium (the latter is the old name for the Roman town of Wroxeter and would have still been inhabited at around this time).

It's not known when the first church was built on this site but it was certainly very early on in Shrewsbury's history. St Chad's was to become very a important church locally with visitors from far and wide. Those visitors had to be accommodated somewhere and so, like the Dun Cow Inn near the Abbey, the Golden Cross Inn was built to serve such people. I'm sure it will come as no surprise to hear that, again like the Dun Cow Inn, this pub, too, is haunted by an old monk.

14. Continue to walk to the end of the street and then turn right towards Belmont. Ahead of you, you will see a tall Georgian building with a remarkable timber-framed gable end with, just on the corner in front, a No Entry sign ahead of you. Obey the sign by turning to your left to walk down Belmont Bank. This street is partially cobbled and can be very slippery when it's wet. Walk down Belmont Bank, past the car parks of the Prince Rupert and Lion Hotels and then turn left under an archway into Barracks Passage.

Barracks Passage is so-called because it was here, in 1485, that many of Henry Tudor's soldiers stayed in the town. Henry Tudor was on his way across England to fight against the king, Richard III. The battle took place in Leicestershire at Bosworth Field. As a result of his victory, Henry became King Henry VII of England, finally uniting both England and Wales under one king.

Many of his men were killed at that battle. For some reason some of them seem to have returned to Shrewsbury in order to haunt this part of the town. One can only assume that the Shrewsbury people had been so hospitable towards these men (the town does, after all, have a reputation as being one of the "politest in England") that they decided to come back here for the rest of time.

15. At the end of Barracks Passage you will go under another archway. This is part of Henry Tudor house, which is so-called because it was here that Henry stayed. When you come into Wyle Cop turn to the right in order to walk down the street towards the English Bridge and then back to the car park beside the Abbey.

Walk 8: Bayston Hill
Shropshire's oldest ghost?

Distance and time: 5 miles (8km); 2.5 hours.

Starting point: Burgs Lane, Baystone Hill, OS reference 489085 .

Maps: Landranger Map 126 or Explorer Map 241.

Terrain: Much of this walk goes along country lanes. Please note that the path crosses over a railway line at one point. There are 12 stiles.

Refreshments and toilets: None on the walk. There are numerous pubs in Bayston Hill.

Introduction

There must be ghosts all over the country that have been around since time immemorial. But there can be few as old as the Roman soldier who is sometimes seen near to Bomere Pool. He must surely rank as one of Shropshire's oldest ghosts.

The walk

The walk starts from Burgs Lane which lies off the A49 (Hereford Road) to the south of the village of Bayston Hill. It leads towards some private houses and to Bayston Farm; care should be taken to park along the roadside in such a way as not to impede any farm or other vehicles.

1. Walk along Burgs Lane, passing the private houses in a north-easterly direction. Just beyond the last house, you will see a footpath ahead of you. As you walk along this footpath look out for a stile that takes you into the field on the right. Directly ahead, you will see a second stile right in front of the railway line with another stile beyond.

   Do take care crossing the track – this is a main line route between Shrewsbury and Hereford.

2. Having crossed the railway line and the stile beyond it, look

ahead and slightly to your right and you will see the next stile on the skyline. Beyond this stile (an old one beside the open field entrance) you will enter a field – walk along this field keeping the hedge line immediately on your right. At the end of this hedge, the field area opens up so that you now find yourself walking with the hedge on your left. The next stile is in this second hedge line on your left. Walk up the hill to the far end of the field where a further stile brings you onto a tarmac farm lane.

3. Turn right to walk along the lane. Just as the lane is about to enter Bomere Farm, you will see signposts directing you over a stile on the left. Just beyond this stile, there are two further stiles, after which you turn to the right. At this point, you will find yourself on the top of a steep slope walking around the outside of all the farm buildings that are to your right. Walk along the top of this slope, at the end of which there is another stile.

This last stile brings you onto a farm track which bears steeply downhill. However, if you look across the track you will see yet another stile to be crossed. In other words, you are constantly walking around the outside of all the farm buildings until you finally come to the southern side of Bomere Farm.

At this point you will see a stile at the entrance to Bomere Wood with, beside it, a sign that says "Please keep to the public footpath". The footpath is clearly defined all the way through the forest with two further stiles along the way.

The best time to see Bomere Pool is when there are no leaves on the trees as the area is quite thickly wooded. There are many small tracks leading down to the pool, used by fishermen and I am sure they all are hoping to catch that really large elusive fish.

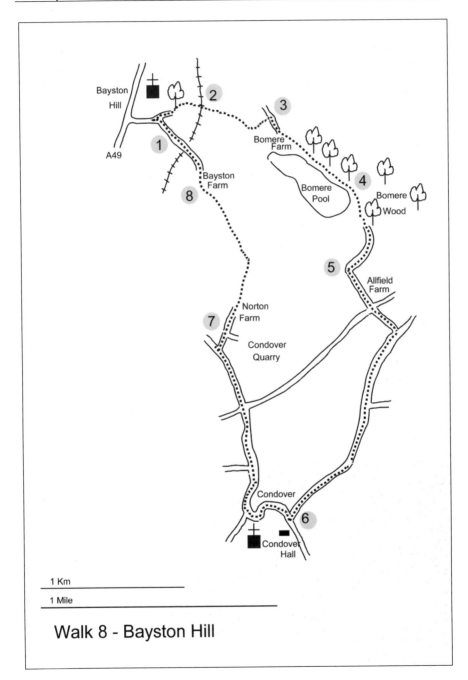

Bayston
Hill

A49

2

3

1

Bomere
Farm

Bayston
Farm

8

Bomere
Pool

4

Bomere
Wood

5

Allfield
Farm

Norton
Farm

7

Condover
Quarry

Condover

6

Condover
Hall

1 Km

1 Mile

Walk 8 - Bayston Hill

In fact there is said to be an enormous fish that lives in this pool. This fish wears a magnificent sword in a sheath attached to its belt. On one occasion the fish was actually caught but managed to escape by slashing at the fisherman's net with his sword until he got away. A "one that got away" story to beat all the best fishermen's tales, I think!

The fish doesn't live here on his own, however. Don't be surprised if you should see a Roman soldier as you walk here, although your best chance of seeing him would be on the eve of Easter. The first Christians in Britain were converted during Roman times. The people who lived here were converted to the new religion but they soon reverted to their old, pagan ways and so this soldier came to try to reconvert them once more. He fell in love with the governor's daughter, who was the only one to accept Christianity again.

God, however, was angry that all the other people refused to follow him and so he sent a flood that drowned the entire settlement – thus forming Bomere Pool. The governor's daughter was amongst those who drowned and the heart-broken soldier went looking for her. Sadly his boat sank and he, too, drowned. Ever since then, when Easter falls on the anniversary of his death, he can be seen still looking for his lost love.

4. Keeping to the main track through the wood along the top of the hill, you will eventually find yourself on a narrow footpath with a conifer hedge and private garden on your right and an old wooden fence on your left. This footpath emerges, over the final stile of the walk, onto a concrete track.

    Incidentally, if you should happen to hear the roar of motorbikes as you are walking through the forest, a sound that is so loud that you fear you are just about to find yourself in the middle of a race track, don't worry. There is indeed a motocross race track here but the walk goes around the site.

5. Follow the concrete track until you reach a crossroads beside Allfield Farm at which point you walk straight on. At the next junction, a T-junction, you will find yourself on a country lane, where you turn right to walk towards Condover.

    Just as you enter the village of Condover you will see, on the other side of the road, the entrance to Condover Hall. Now used as a school for blind children it was built in 1598 and is one of the finest Elizabethan houses in Shropshire. Local legend tells us that that fish that swims in Bomere Pool will give up the beautiful sword that it wears to the rightful owner of Condover Hall whenever he should return. There are obviously tales of alleged skulduggery here but no-one seems to know what gave rise to this legend, nor how long ago the rightful heir to the estate was cheated from his birthright.

6. On entering Condover turn to the right. There is no pavement along the first section of the road and so care should be taken while walking along here. Walk through the village bearing right at the road junction following the sign to Bayston Hill and follow this road for nearly half a mile until you come to the entrance to Norton Farm and Condover Quarry. Although a private road the public footpath goes along the length of this road until, where the road turns sharply right to enter Norton Farm the footpath goes straight on. At this point, you will see a public footpath sign to confirm that you are, indeed, on the correct route.

It was in the gravel pits here that the skeletons of four mammoths were found not long ago. They are now on display at the Shropshire Hills Discovery Centre in Craven Arms.

From this point on the walk you will have an excellent view of Lyth Hill towards the west. There is treasure buried under that hill somewhere, or so it is said!

Once upon a time there was a gnome who lived under the

Condover Hall

hill and he came up above ground one day and fell into conversation with a shepherd. The shepherd invited the gnome to stay with him and the gnome replied that he would stay for seven days after which, if he liked the life, he would either stay forever to go back underground forever. Now the shepherd had a beautiful sister and the gnome fell in love with her. At the end of the seven days, when the shepherd asked him if he had come to a decision, the gnome replied that he would like to stay above the ground, but only if he could marry the shepherd's sister.

The gnome was kind and gentle but he was also old and ugly and the shepherd had hoped to marry his sister off to a wealthy prince. But when he told his sister what the gnome had said she replied that she would like to marry him and so the shepherd agreed that the gnome could marry his sister.

Before the wedding, however, the gnome returned briefly to his underground home to collect all that he would need to build a fine home for his bride and, when he returned, he was laden with gold and jewels and beautiful things which he also shared with the shepherd. All three lived happily ever after but there remains, to this day, somewhere under Lyth Hill, that part of the gnome's treasure that he couldn't carry with him when he returned that day long ago.

7. After leaving the track the footpath enters a large field, with the hedge line on your immediate right. Take care at this point because, within 100 metres you will come to a large gap in the hedge at which point you want to continue walking straight on but, from here on, keeping the hedge line on your left. At the far end of the field there is a metal gate, which leads into a further field. From here, you walk directly towards Bayston Farm at the other end of the field.

8. The path takes you around the left-hand side of Bayston Farm and on to a tarmac lane. This is Burgs Lane once more and, from here, you follow the lane back to your car.

Walk 9: Earl's Hill
A hilltop battlefield

Distance and time: 5 miles (8km); 3 hours.

Starting point: Car park at Poles Coppice Nature Reserve, OS reference 393048.

Maps: Landranger Map 126 or Explorer Maps 216 and 241.

Terrain: Although this is a relatively short walk, the climb up and down Earl's Hill is very steep. Coming down the hill is extremely hazardous as there is a lot of loose gravel and great care should be taken. There are five stiles.

Refreshments and toilets: The Mytton Arms in Habberley and several pubs in Pontesbury.

Introduction

A clear landmark from many directions Earl's Hill is topped with an old Iron Age hill fort that may have been reused by Saxon warlords giving rise to a number of local legends.

The walk

Park in the car park for Poles Coppice Nature Reserve at the end of Pontesbury Hill Road.

1. Walk back along the road towards Pontesbury until you come to a bridleway along a gravel track where you turn to the right, signposted to Poles Coppice. Walk along this track for about 500 metres and look out for a metal gate on the right through which the bridleway continues onto a grass track – the signpost is almost lost against a holly bush. This track leads to open grassland behind some recently restored cottages at Nills Farm. Walk onto the gravel car park that serves the houses, through the old farmyard and onto a tarmac drive, walking east. Where the drive meets a country road cross the road to enter a field through a kissing gate.

2. The footpath will leave this field via a stile in the far right-hand corner. However, the path itself follows the hedge line, first walking directly ahead and then turning right at the far end of the field. After crossing the stile, keep to the right-hand side of the next fields, crossing over two further stiles in order to reach the track beyond.

3. Turn to the left. This track starts as a gravelled track, passes several houses and finally emerges as a tarmac road. At the first road junction keep to the right, walking around Pontesford Hill until you reach the Pontesford Hill car park, which you enter.

4. At the other side of the car park there is a clearly defined track climbing up Pontesford Hill towards the small hill fort at the northern end. Just as you reach the hill fort there is a track to the left climbing steeply up the hill; it is identified by a post with green and brown arrows on it. The track climbs steeply and eventually comes to a stile where it leaves the forest. Beyond the stile, the path continues up to the top of Earl's Hill where there is a trig point and a magnificent 360 degrees view.

There is a haunted yew tree on the top of Pontesford Hill, though which tree it is, it is a bit difficult to tell these days. There used to be a tradition on Palm Sunday that young people from Pontesbury would race to get to the tree first in order to pick a branch from it and so be assured of good luck for the coming year. Those of them who weren't married could then discover who their future partners would be by racing from the tree, down the hill to a nearby brook where there was a bottomless pool of water. The first person to reach this pool would then dip the fourth finger of his or her left-hand in the water and the very next person of the opposite sex that he or she met would be their future spouse.

Once you reach the open ground near the top of Earl's Hill you also get your first clear impression of the military potential of this hilltop site. The earthworks of the Iron Age hill fort can be seen most clearly to the south and west and the path continues through them. There was once a battle here, or so the story goes, between two Saxon kings one of whom had presumably seen the advantage of refortifying the site. During the course of the battle one of the kings shot an

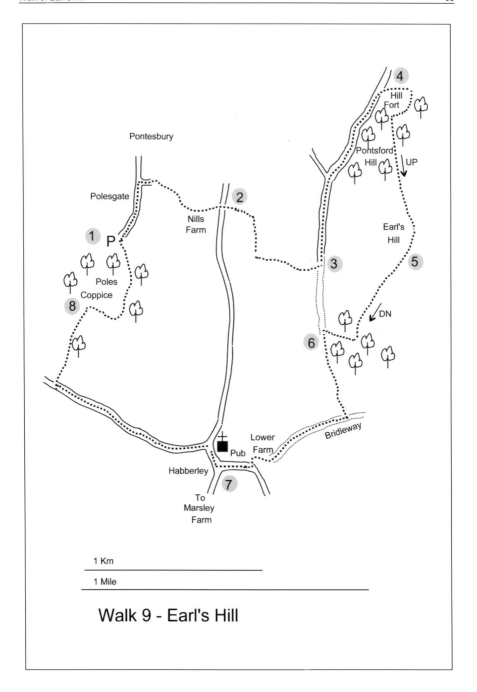

1 Km

1 Mile

Walk 9 - Earl's Hill

arrow made of solid gold but in the melee it was lost. Whosoever finds that arrow is assured of great wealth (naturally!) and good fortune.

In fact the Shropshire writer, Mary Webb, used this legend as the background to her first book, The Golden Arrow, which was published in 1916. Mary Webb lived for a time in Pontesbury.

5. Continue walking to the south through the ancient ramparts. At first, the slope is quite gentle but it soon becomes very steep indeed. It is important that you take extreme care while descending here as there is a great deal of loose gravel lying on the surface of the ground which it would be easy to slip on. Finally, you reach the forest once more, entering it over a stile. At the T-junction immediately beyond the stile, follow the path to the right.

6. The path meets a trackway that goes along the bottom of the hill; turn left through the metal gate walking south. At the next gate the track ends and becomes a footpath going straight ahead through two fields, leaving the second field through another gate onto a bridleway where you turn right. This is part of a route known as the Marches Way. Follow the bridleway to Lower Farm, walk through the farmyard and turn right when you meet the tarmac road into the village of Habberley.

In the village the route goes past the Mytton Arms pub on the right. It is named for a well-known Shropshire family whose most famous (or infamous) member was John Mytton, who lived near Whittington. There are so many stories about him. Most people have heard that a sudden shock is supposed to be an excellent cure for hiccups. Well, "Mad Jack" Mytton, as he was known, was never a man for half measures over anything. One day, when he woke up, he began to hiccup. How could he give himself a sudden shock to get rid of them? He came up with an excellent idea – he would set fire to his bedclothes that would surely cure the hiccups. However, he ended up with severe burns himself. The story doesn't relate whether or not he actually managed to cure his hiccups in this way. One must assume that he did!

Just as you come to the church there is a lane leading south which goes past Marsley Farm. Local tradition has it that this farm sits

Earl's Hill

on the site of a hunting lodge that once belonged to King Ethelred the Unready, who reigned at the turn of the 10th and 11th centuries. The man who lived here at that time was a man called Aedric who owned many manors in the county of Shropshire. He was, however, such a nasty piece of work that "he makes Attila the Hun look like Mother Teresa" according to some local people.

Aedric married a daughter of King Ethelred. He was extremely ambitious and saw no reason why he, himself, should not be king of England. He began to climb the ladder towards his goal, killing his way to the top. Eventually only the new king, Canute, stood between him and his ambitions but it was Canute who this time wielded the knife first and Aedric who died.

7. Beyond the pub follow the road signs for Minsterley, turning right at the first junction (beside the church) and left at the second. The road climbs steadily uphill for just over half a mile before you come to a footpath leading to the north (to the right) along a small track. This opens up, through a metal kissing gate, into a field. Continue walking north, keeping to the left of the

Poles Coppice

copse of trees that is straight ahead. From here, there are views of the Welsh hills to the west and Earl's Hill to the east, with perhaps the clearest view of the old ramparts.

8.   On entering Poles Coppice through a wooden kissing gate bear sharp right following the footpath that is indicated by a yellow arrow footpath sign. This leads down the hillside before turning sharply left in the valley. Follow the path by going straight ahead until you reach the car park again.

Walk 10: Chirbury
A king's boundary

Distance and time: 6 miles (10km); 3.5 hours.

Starting point: The village of Chirbury. There are no official car parks in the village and so you will need to park somewhere along the road in the village. Please therefore park with due consideration to other people, especially to anyone who may be wanting to use the village shop.

Maps: Landranger Map 137 or Explorer Map 216.

Terrain: This is a relatively easy walk although walking boots are advisable since you will be walking through some farm yards. There are nine stiles altogether.

Refreshments and toilets: There are none on the walk. There is one pub in Chirbury, the Herbert Arms, and further pubs, coffee shops and public toilets in Montgomery.

Introduction

When King Offa built his Dyke at the end of the 8th century it was intended as a boundary between the English and the Welsh. Only a few sections of the dyke still mark the English/Welsh border and one such section is included in this walk so that, for the length of one field only, this walk enters Wales.

The walk

The walk starts from the church in the centre of the village, next to the Herbert Arms pub.

Should you be taking this walk on the last day of October, Halloween, it might be an idea to test out a local legend. It is said that if anyone walks around the

church twelve times on Halloween then, after the final circuit, a voice will ring out with a list of all those who live in the parish who are due to die in the coming year.

One year a local man did just that. He walked around the church twelve times and then, at the end, he heard a voice. Contrary to your expectations, that voice did not ring out with his own name. Instead, the name that was mentioned was that of one of his close friends. The man went to his friend with the sad news of his imminent demise but the friend laughed and said he didn't believe in such nonsense. But the truth must be told, and, sure enough, that friend was dead before another year had gone by.

None of the versions of this story that I have come across seems to stipulate whether you should walk around the church in a clockwise or anti-clockwise direction. Such details, however, are usually very important in these old legends. Consequently, if you walk around the church the full twelve times and don't hear the voice then it has to be assumed that you were walking in the wrong direction. There will be nothing for it, then, but to repeat the exercise in the opposite direction. If you still fail to hear the voice at the end, then you can perhaps safely assume that no-one in the parish is due to meet his or her death in the coming twelve months.

If, after all that exercise, you still feel capable of continuing with the walk, you should proceed as follows.

1. Coming out of the churchyard turn right along the main road (the A490) towards Welshpool, walking along the road for about one third of a mile. Take care along this stretch of road as there is no pavement here. The road narrows to cross a small bridge and then, begins to climb slightly. At this point, there is a footpath sign leading off to the left into a field.

2. The path follows a gravel track along the right-hand side of the field. This track goes through three fields before petering out to become a footpath. You are heading towards Winsbury Farm, your view of which will be dominated by the tall silo standing beside the farm. As you walk towards the farm, in each field keep to the right-hand side of the field, until you reach the third stile beside a metal gate, which comes out at the right-hand side of all the farm buildings.

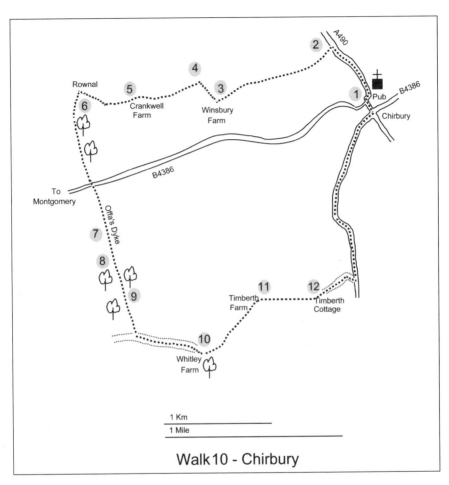

Walk 10 - Chirbury

3. Coming over the third stile you find yourself on a Permissive Path with a yellow arrow sign on it. The original footpath would have gone through the farm yard at this point, but now there is a track around the farm buildings. This bears to the left where you will see a clearly defined gravel track going down the hill towards a metal gate. Follow this track and, as you pass through the gate, look to the left of the field and you will see a wooden structure in the hedge. This is a wooden bridge and it has a yellow arrow sign on it to confirm that you are on the correct route.

4. As you leave the bridge, the exit from this field is at the far right-hand side of the field under a tall oak tree, just to the left of a metal gate – it is over another wooden bridge. From here, you are heading for the next farm, Crankwell Farm, again dominated by a tall silo. When you reach the farm walk around it, keeping the farm buildings on your left and you will find yourself on a gravel track.

5. Just beyond the farm the gravel track forks – take the track that bears to the left. It goes through a gap in a hedge and then enters a large field beyond. In this field, walk diagonally towards the far right-hand corner where you will find a stile, beyond which there is a another gravel track, this time leading to the right to Rownal. Walk in this direction.

6. As you reach Rownal, a private house, walk past the garage and then immediately turn left. You will then see a sign for the Offa's Dyke Path (a blue arrow with an acorn symbol on it) directing you to the left once more through a gate and up into a field beside the dyke. Before you reach the end of this field you will see a gap in the earthworks on your right, allowing you to cross over the rampart so that you can then follow the route of the dyke on the other side. Following the Offa's Dyke Path will take you across the main road that links Chirbury and Montgomery (the B4386) where you will use a stile to enter the next field.

It is at this point that the enormity of the project for building the Dyke finally becomes apparent. I am always particularly fascinated by the thought of the logistics required for building such a structure. This part of the country is not very thickly populated to begin with. In those days, over 1200 years ago, the population must have been sparse indeed. Certainly there was nothing like the manpower necessary to build such a structure available locally.

This was no problem for King Offa, however. His realm extended from here all the way east to the North Sea. The Mersey and Trent Rivers would have formed his northern borders. To the south, London was within his territory, as were the counties of Kent and Surrey and Sussex and also, possibly, parts of Hampshire. His only rival in the region was the kingdom of Wessex to the south-west. Offa certainly could call on the necessary manpower to build his dyke.

However, the men who actually worked on the building of the dyke must have had to travel here from their villages and hamlets around the country. While they were here, they would have required food and at least a basic form of shelter. It's sad that the stories of these individuals don't survive today.

7. The Offa's Dyke Path takes you through a pen with gates on either side. Beyond the pen climb up onto the rampart of the dyke to enjoy the best view of Montgomery.

Although in neighbouring Wales today and, obviously, on the Welsh side of the border in King Offa's time, there have been periods in its history when Montgomery was considered as part of the county of Shropshire. It is a very attractive small town and thrived particularly in the 18th century at the time of stage coach travel when it was an important stop for coaches travelling into central Wales.

The town is dominated by its castle and, from this position, it is possible to clearly see its keep with the moat around it and the modern footbridge into the castle where once there would have been a drawbridge. As border castles go in this region, this one wasn't built until comparatively late. The first castle in the area was a wooden castle built at nearby Hen Domen nearer to the Severn Valley where the castle's custodian could watch all the comings and goings at Rhydwhyman, the point on the river where the English traditionally met the Welsh for trade and even, on occasion, to make treaties.

The stone castle, however, dates from the early 1200s when it was built on the orders of King Henry III. It was from this period, also, that the town of Montgomery began to develop. The castle was finally demolished during the Civil War in the 1600s.

From this viewpoint, also, it is possible to see the tower of St Nicholas's church. In the churchyard lies the Robber's Grave. John Davies, whose grave it is, was a highwayman in the district. He was captured and tried for his crimes, found guilty and sentenced to be hanged. However, he vehemently proclaimed his innocence of all charges and, when going to his execution in 1821 he predicted that, as a sign that he was indeed innocent, no grass would grow on his grave for 20 years after he was buried.

And, sure enough, no grass grew on his grave for 20 years!

In fact, it's said that when some people tried to make the grass grow by deliberately planting seeds on the grave they were paralysed or else died soon afterwards, themselves.

8.   The footpath then leads you off the ramparts in order to cross through a stile, after which you will find yourself walking along beside the dyke, on the Welsh side. For the remainder of the time that this walk follows the route of the dyke, it also serves as the English-Welsh border so that, for the length of this field you are walking in Wales itself. At the end of the field you come to another stile which sits beside a gap in the dyke so that you cross over the dyke here and continue to walk, once more in England, still following all the signs for the Offa's Dyke Path.

In the years after the dyke had first been built it would have been rather dangerous for a Welshman to be found on this side of it. For example, it is quite legal to kill a Welshman on a Sunday in Hereford, provided that the killing is done within the area of the Cathedral Close and the weapon used is a longbow which is fired from a distance of exactly 12 yards. The law that states all this dates from over 1000 years ago and has never been repealed.

Supposedly, any Welshman found on the wrong side of the dyke was liable to have a hand cut off which seems a bit extreme. Having a hand cut off was a punishment for theft in those long-ago days and perhaps it was also used for cattle rustlers – which brings to mind a certain nursery rhyme:

> Taffy was a Welshman, Taffy was a thief,
> Taffy came to my house and stole a piece of beef;
> I went to Taffy's house, Taffy wasn't in,
> I jumped upon his Sunday hat, and poked it with a pin.

Many of our nursery rhymes refer to actual events of the past and this one is a direct reference to cattle rustling in the Welsh Marches. It was obviously written by an Englishman! But it's interesting to note that, although in every verse the Welsh get accused of the worse crime, the English obviously retaliated when they got the opportunity!

9. Continue walking along the route of the Offa's Dyke Path, crossing two further stiles, until you reach a tarmac lane that goes through the dyke. At this point, turn left to walk along the lane to Whitley Farm. Walk through the farmyard (there are gates on either side of the yard) and then through a third gate beyond which is a small copse with fenced area for the breeding of pheasants.

10. As you enter the copse you will see a blue arrow sign directing you to the left. This path leads through another gate and into a field. Follow the track that you will see in the field; it soon becomes a gravelled track leading to Timberth Farm. This section of the track can be very messy as cows use it to walk to their milking parlours.

11. At Timberth Farm you walk through a gate and bear right to pass through a second gate. Walk around the back of the farmhouse, bearing right. Just beyond the farmhouse, you will see two trees (very tall pear trees). Walk between these trees and into the field beyond. In the middle of the field is a telegraph pole with a gate in the hedge line beyond. Go through the gate and then bear left in the next field, heading this time for Timberth Cottage. Just to the left of the cottage there is a gate followed immediately by a stile.

12. You will now find yourself on a gravel road. Walk along this to the tarmac country lane beyond. Turn left and walk along the lane for one mile to return to Chirbury.

Walk 11: Mitchell's Fold
A magical cow

Distance and time: 5 miles (8km); 2.5 hours.

Starting point: Lay-by near Middleton church; OS reference 298993.

Maps: Landranger Map 137 or Explorer Map 216.

Terrain: There is one stile. The walk has a steady climb at the beginning but, otherwise, it is easy walking.

Refreshments and toilets: There are none on the walk. The Old Miner's Arms at Priest Weston and The Herbert Arms in Chirbury are both nearby.

Introduction

Versions of the legend of the dun cow are to be found in many parts of England. It features a cow that ran amok through the countryside and was eventually killed by Earl Guy of Warwick many miles away, just outside the town of Warwick. The story, however, is said to have started in Shropshire.

The walk

Park in the lay-by that is to be found between Middleton Hall Farm and the church to the north.

1. Walk south, past the farm before turning left along a tarmac lane, following a brown sign to the Stone Circle. After a few hundred metres, just beyond a turning into a farm on the left, there is a footpath sign beside a stile into a field on the left. Keeping to the right-hand side of the field, walk up to the top where there is a gate into open land beyond. The route now follows a clearly defined grassy track through bracken, always climbing uphill and veering towards the left.

    The views looking back towards Wales are superb as you reach the top. On the left of the path, Pillow Mounds are identified on the Ordnance Survey map at this point. They are, in fact, the remains of

Norman rabbit warrens dug here nearly 1,000 years ago. The rabbit was actually introduced to England by the Normans as a readily available, year-long source of food.

2. From here a stone cairn can be seen on the skyline to the east. Use this as a marker to head for, ignoring other paths and a small stream along the way. The cairn will disappear briefly as you walk towards it but the path is well defined. Eventually the path starts to aim slightly to the left of the cairn; continue to follow it until you meet another footpath along the crest of the hill when you turn right to reach the cairn itself.

From here the views towards the east can finally be enjoyed. Ahead are the Stiperstones Hills with the jagged outline of the Devil's Chair clearly defined. Down in the valley below runs the road linking Shrewsbury and Bishop's Castle and the ruins of two buildings over the shafts to old lead mines can be seen. One is to the south beside the road and one is directly ahead, just in front of the conifer forest on Shelve Hill – perhaps Wild Edric lies buried somewhere near here.

3. From the stone cairn continue walking to the south, turning right when you reach a junction with another footpath. At the next junction turn left, you are now walking along a grassy all-vehicle track towards Mitchell's Fold itself.

Mitchell's Fold is an ancient Bronze Age Circle, built probably around 3,500 years ago. Compared to better known circles around Britain this is very small but there may have been up to 30 stones here originally. Today only 15 stones survive and they still form a clearly defined circle.

Mitchell's Fold stone circle

As with other circles the theories as to why it was built and for what purpose abound. But here in Shropshire we know just why this one exists.

The people who lived here long, long ago had a hard life just to survive. Then one day a kindly fairy appeared and gave them a magic cow.

"You need never be worried by famine again", said the fairy to the local people, "for this cow will always provide you with milk."

Unfortunately a wicked fairy arrived in the neighbourhood soon afterwards and started to milk the cow herself. She milked that cow and she milked that cow and, try as it might, the poor cow just could not fill her bucket. Because, you see, the wicked fairy was using a bucket with a hole in it. Eventually the cow went berserk and ran off through the countryside terrorising everyone until, eventually, it was killed by Earl Guy in Warwickshire.

Meanwhile, the good fairy returned and, as though by magic, a circle of stones appeared within which the wicked fairy was imprisoned, never to work her evil again. Some people say that she was turned into stone herself, imprisoned within the circle. Or, perhaps, her stone might be the solitary one lying beyond the circle that you will see on your left in the bracken as you continue with your walk.

4. Leaving Mitchell's Fold continue along the path to the south through a kissing gate onto a gravel track. On reaching the tarmac road turn to the right towards Priest Weston, and start to walk downhill. At this point, the road to the village runs parallel to the English-Welsh border with Wales in the fields to the south. Just beyond a road sign indicating a steep slope, turn to the right along a tarmac track between two gates. This track passes a small group of houses, becoming a gravel track.

The track makes a sharp left-hand turn at which point there is a grassy track leading directly ahead with a yellow arrow sign beside it. Follow the grass lane, an old sunken routeway, which leads directly to the village of Priest Weston.

Priest Weston was the birthplace of John Brunt, a man who in an earlier age would, by now, have become the hero of a local legend. Even as a young boy he was quite fearless and it's said that, at this time,

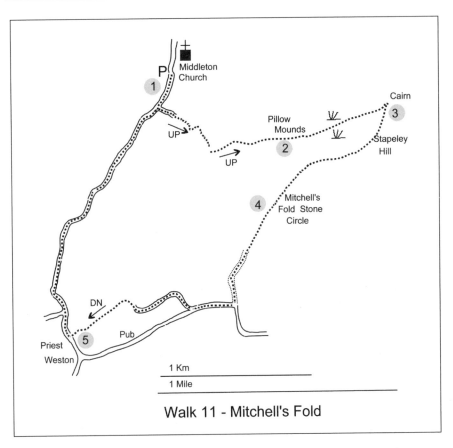

Walk 11 - Mitchell's Fold

his hero was Mad Jack Mytton whom he would try to emulate by riding any animal he came across.

Soon after the Second World War broke out he joined the army and, in 1944, he was in Italy when his battalion came under severe attack by a German Panzer Division. With their anti-tank defences and their own tanks destroyed, and fiercely outnumbered, the men were finally ordered to withdraw. Brunt stayed behind to give the other men covering fire until, out of ammunition, he dashed to a new position. This aggressive defence caused the enemy soldiers to pause in their fighting giving Brunt the opportunity to take a party of men back to their earlier position in order to save wounded soldiers who had been left there.

Captain Brunt was awarded a VC for his heroism that day. Sadly, he was killed the following day while standing drinking tea back at his platoon headquarters when a stray shell landed beside him.

5. In the village turn to the right when you reach the road. You will soon come to a road junction, go straight ahead, following the sign to Marton and Shrewsbury. This road leads all the way back to the lay-by near Middleton church.

Middleton Church

But first, before you climb back in your car and go home, you must visit the church. The church was built in 1842 and, at first, appears nothing out of the ordinary. However, in 1872 a young clergyman named Waldegrave Brewster arrived and he soon embarked on the task of adorning his new church by carving the pew ends. When the pews had been completed, he carved the stone corbels by the north transept with pictures of the legend of Mitchell's Fold. There you can see two girls arriving to milk the cow with their buckets in their hands. The witch is also shown milking the cow with her tall witch's hat on her head; even the stones of the circle that imprisoned the witch can be seen. It is a total delight.

Carved pew end

Walk 12: The Stiperstones
Where the Devil sits

Distance and time: 6 miles (9km); 3 hours.

Shorter route: 3 miles (5km); 1.5 hours.

Starting point: Stiperstones Car Park; OS reference 369977.

Maps: Landranger Map 137 or Explorer Map 216.

Terrain: There are 13 stiles (even agile dogs may need help with a few of them). Some steady climbs and sections of the walk will be soggy after heavy rainfall. It's very rocky between Cranberry Rock and the Devil's Chair – this is not a section to be walked when the ground is snow-covered and you can't see where you are putting your feet. The shorter walk is suitable for children.

Refreshments and toilets: None on the walk. The Bog Field Centre, the Horseshoe Inn at Bridges and Stiperstones Inn at Stiperstones can all be found nearby. The Bog Field Centre is only open in the summer months – there is a tea-room here and the centre has displays on the geology, history and legends of the region that make it well worth a visit.

Introduction

It is said that the Devil hates England more than any other country in the world for he knows that we are good Protestants and read the Bible. However, if he could make the Stiperstones sink into the bowels of the Earth, England would be no more. And so he sits on his chair hoping that his weight will be enough to sink the hill and all the land around!

The walk

To follow the shorter route cross through the gate beside the car park that leads directly up to the top of the hill. Walk past the Cranberry Rock outcrop on your left following the main, clearly defined, path. Join the directions for the long walk at point 6.

1.   Start the long walk by crossing the road at the entrance to the car

park. Directly opposite is a stile with a narrow footpath. The path is very overgrown with gorse and there is barbed wire along the top of the fence so watch where you put your hands.

Follow this path straight ahead through a small, iron gate, across the entrance to Knolls Farm and across another stile at the bottom left-hand corner of the field. Across this stile the ground can be quite marshy; keep towards the left-hand side of the field and you will find a wooden bridge with the third stile; continue straight on, crossing a fourth stile into a tarmac lane. Turn left, to walk downhill.

2. Pass two cottages on the right-hand side. The second is Knolls Cottage and immediately beyond it there is a footpath sign and stile up on the bank of the road leading to the right. At the end of the path cross over a further stile into a field. Climb uphill, keeping to the left of the field. Do NOT cross over the old stile at the top left of the field. Instead walk a few yards to your right and you will find a further stile with a yellow arrow on it. Cross this stile – a rather steep stile, difficult for those of us with short legs!

Almost immediately you will see a gravel path – turn left. At the next junction bear left again. This section of the path can get very muddy after sustained rain. After a few minutes, you will move from relatively open forest into darker, planted pine forest. Keep straight on. In the pine forest, there are occasional route markers to keep you on track.

3. Eventually you come to a T-junction with a clearly defined gravel track. This is the Shropshire Way, which you will now follow for most of the walk. Turn right, up the hill.

Hidden amongst rubble on the right are the ruins of an old house. People living here in the past would have had a very hard life – they were mainly hill farmers who augmented their income by working in the mines. Lead has been mined here from Roman times with production peaking in the 1800s.

One of the old lead mines hereabouts is reputed to be where Wild Edric lies buried. Edric was a Saxon lord who rebelled against the Norman invaders. He has been seen many times in recent centuries,

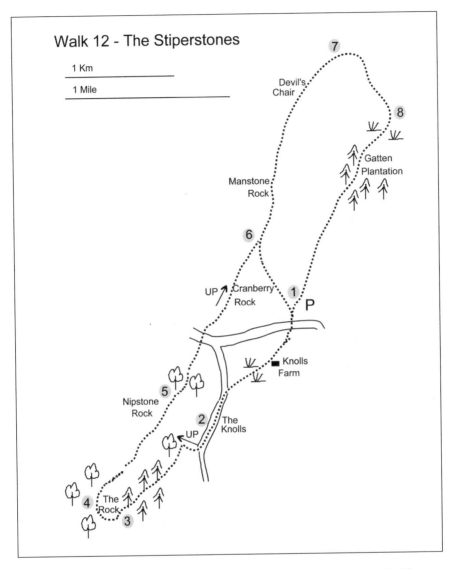

Walk 12 - The Stiperstones

1 Km

1 Mile

riding about the countryside on his white charger accompanied by hunting dogs. When he is seen it's a warning of a national disaster, a warning (in other words) that the country is about to go to war. And if you count the dogs running ahead of him that will tell you for how many years the war will last.

If, however, he is only heard but not seen at all, then it is a warning of a personal disaster. I met an elderly lady once whose mother had heard Wild Edric many years before. The lady's mother was walking along a road when she heard a horseman riding quickly along the track behind her. She moved out of the way of the galloping horse, she felt the horse's breath on her cheeks as it passed by. But she never saw a thing. The following year, 11 members of her family died.

4. Just beyond The Rock the path forks. The Shropshire Way is clearly marked going to the right. There are a number of tracks in the forest, keep bearing right, following the Shropshire Way markers (with a silhouette of a bird of prey) until you leave the forest into open heath land.

You now start to enjoy the views that make this walk so worth while. Looking to the south-west you will see Corndon Hill and, to the east, the long, flat Long Mynd. You may see gliders taking off from the Midlands Gliding Club on the top of the Mynd. Walk northwards, passing the Nipstone Rock to the left and crossing over a Forestry Commission gravel track.

This is also a good place, in the early autumn, to hunt for cranberries which grow all over the hillsides amongst the heather. The Shropshire name for them is "whinberries" and, until relatively recently, when they were ripe local schools would close so that the children could be sent on the hills to pick them.

5. Re-enter the forest just beyond the track, still clearly sign posted. The path goes straight along the edge of the forest, cross-ing over three stiles to enter an open field. A line of scattered trees roughly marks the right-hand side of the path. Go straight ahead, towards the jagged rock on the skyline. At the end of the field cross over two further stiles with a tarmac road between. A few yards on climb over a further stile – this one is marked with a "Wild Edric's Way" sign. You have now entered the Stiperstones National Nature Reserve. Climb uphill and, wherever the paths appear to diverge, follow the one that leads to the rock outcrop on the top of the hill, Cranberry Rock.

As you approach Cranberry Rock the Shropshire Way path bears to the left around the tor. When you reach what seems like

The Devil's Chair

a "river of rocks" crossing your path the footing is easiest if you bear slightly left. The path around Cranberry Rock often seems quite small and ill-defined. Follow this path until it joins the main path coming up from the car park down below on the right. – the two paths join just below Manstone Rock which is easily identifiable because it has a trig point on the top.

It has been predicted that Wild Edric will come back to life when we, once again, have an English King on the throne. He's been waiting a long time. After all, to a Saxon like Edric the Tudors would have been too Welsh and the Stuarts, too Scots. He would probably consider even our present Queen as being too Scottish. Perhaps he will return when Charles or, more likely, when William becomes King.

The Stiperstones are made up of quartzite rocks formed over 450 million years ago. The spectacular jagged outlines of the rocks are the result of repeated freezing and thawing of ice on the rocks during the last Ice Age which caused them to crack and shatter.

Or you could explain it by saying it's the work of the Devil. Apparently the Devil had had a quarrel with the townspeople of Shrewsbury and he decided to bury the town under a huge heap of rocks. He picked up a pile of rocks and, carrying them in his apron, walked across the hills towards Shrewsbury. But, suddenly, the strings of his apron broke and the rocks fell all over the hillside – where they remain to this day.

6. From this point until just after the Devil's Chair the path becomes increasingly rocky and care needs to be taken to look where you put your feet. The Shropshire Way leads you along to the right of the Manstone Rock before reaching the Devil's Chair rising above you on the left. There are a number of smaller tracks around the tor; keep to the main track heading in a northerly direction at the far right-hand side of the Chair. From this point, the walking becomes much easier.

    If you want to understand why this rocky outcrop has been described as a chair then take a brief detour at the northern end and then look up at it. You will see what looks remarkably like the shape of an armchair where the Devil could easily sit and admire the view looking north.

    Take care which day you decide to go on this walk. There is one day, or rather night, in the year that you would be wise to avoid. That's the night of the 21 December when, each year, all the ghosts of Shropshire meet here for their AGM. The Devil, himself, chairs the meeting from, appropriately enough, the Devil's Chair.

7. When you reach a clearly defined cross roads with a gravel track turn to the right onto the track walking downhill. Although this is still the Shropshire Way there are, at this point, no waymarkers. However, you will soon reach a stone wall with a gate, a stile next to it and a Shropshire Way marker to confirm that you are on the right route. Pass through this gate into an open field. Although not as clear as before, the path is fairly well defined and goes directly downhill with, after a few yards, a wire fenced field enclosed to the left.

8. Towards the bottom of the field there are two signposts to The Knolls and Car Park. Follow these to the right. At the next sign-post you leave the Shropshire Way, crossing over a small stream and then soon enter Gatten Plantation though another gate/stile. Follow this path all the way back to the car park.

Walk 13: The Long Mynd

A prehistoric routeway

Distance and time: 8 miles (13km); 4 hours.

Starting point: By the entrance to Ratlinghope church; OS reference 402969.

Maps: Landranger Map 137 or Explorer Map 217.

Terrain: A steady climb to the top of Long Mynd but the ground underfoot is generally very good although there are some places along the top where the track is severely worn. There are four stiles.

Refreshments and toilets: None on the walk. Horseshoe Pub at Bridges. In summer refreshments can sometimes be obtained at a café in Ratlinghope, next to the church. Alternatively, again only in the summer season, the Bog Field Centre on the other side of the Stiperstones provides teas and information about the region.

Introduction

On a clear summer's day this walk is very rewarding. There are magnificent views in all directions and it's difficult, then, to imagine just how treacherous these hills can be at other times of the year.

The walk

Park by the entrance to Ratlinghope church.

> There is not much room so please park considerately, leaving room for any funeral cortege that may have to reach the church. Don't be surprised if you see one, a very grand affair followed by a large number of villagers. The hearse is draped in black and is drawn by two black horses with plumes on their heads. The cortege has been seen locally many times in the last century. Sometimes it appears in the evening on the top of Long Mynd but more often it will be seen on the road between Ratlinghope and Bridges. Strangely, there is no record of any such funeral taking place here in Victorian times and yet it would appear to have been a very grand funeral indeed.

1. Walk south towards Bridges, turning first left following the sign

to Belmore and Church Stretton, going up the hill until you enter the National Trust land over a cattle grid. Immediately after crossing the cattle grid there is a track to the left sign posted to the Shooting Box. At first, this is a concrete track leading to a house but, as it reaches the house, it turns off to the right up the hill. There are a number of small tracks leading from the main one – but always follow the main track that leads uphill.

This climb is very steady but soon rewards you with excellent views towards the west – a good excuse to stop and get your breath. On a clear summer's day it is difficult to comprehend just how treacherous this terrain can be. The weather here has often proved to be life-threatening. One man who nearly lost his life walking across these hills was Donald Carr – it all happened one night in the 1860s. Donald Carr was the vicar of the parishes of both Woolstaston and Ratlinghope and, after taking the Sunday service in one parish, would then walk to the other to conduct a service there.

He had just finished the service in Ratlinghope and wanted to return to his home in Woolstaston. There was snow falling as he set off and everyone advised him to stay overnight rather than attempt to walk home. But he had walked the route many times and knew it well, or so he thought. He set off over the hills but, within a very short time, was totally lost. For all of that night and the next day (27 hours altogether) he stumbled around the hills, falling into gullies, suffering from snow blindness. At one point he lost one of his shoes and he may have suffered a nasty accident, had he not been found as he stumbled down the hillside.

Revd Carr wrote a book about his "Night in the Snow" the proceeds from the sale of which later paid for carvings in Woolstaston church where he lies buried with his wife.

2. Eventually the track links up with the tarmac road. By this point, the worst of the climb is behind you. On reaching the tarmac leave the footpath and continue up the hill along the roadside. On reaching the car park on the left, walk beyond it for a brief visit to the Shooting Box.

The Shooting Box was built as a hide for grouse shooting. Another bump in the landscape here is an old Bronze Age burial mound and there are several others along the crest of the Long Mynd.

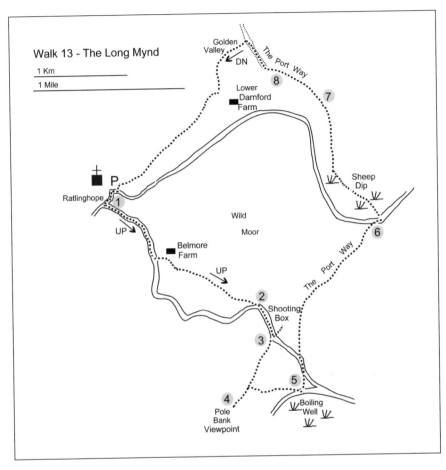

Walk 13 - The Long Mynd

1 Km

1 Mile

Golden Valley

DN

The Port Way

8

7

Lower Darnford Farm

P

Ratlinghope

1

UP

Belmore Farm

UP

Wild

Moor

Sheep Dip

6

The Port Way

2

Shooting Box

3

The Port Way

5

4

Pole Bank Viewpoint

Boiling Well

Incidentally, the name 'mynd' means mountain and the Long Mountain exactly describes it, a long, flat-topped mountain extending for about 8 miles.

3. On leaving the Shooting Box walk back towards the car park and then cross the tarmac road to walk directly south along a track through the heather. As you walk south, you will see the trig point at Pole Bank on the skyline, usually clearly defined by the number of people who stop there to admire the view. In fact, just beside the trig point is a toposcope that was erected in 1986 to mark the jubilee of the Council for the Protection of Rural

England, which tells you that you are now 517m above sea level. You have climbed 242m since leaving Ratlinghope.

At this point you are also following the route of the Jack Mytton Way. A totally spoilt child who grew up to be a drunken wastrel, Jack Mytton has since come to be known as one of Shropshire's more beloved eccentrics. The Jack Mytton Way is a bridleway route dedicated to his memory – he was an

The toposcope at Pole Bank

extremely accomplished horseman and keen hunter. Indeed it's said that he used to train his horses for hunting by riding them up and down the staircases within his home at Halston Hall in the north of Shropshire.

One day Mad Jack was riding in his gig with a friend when he asked his friend if he had ever been upset in one. When the friend replied, "No", Jack exclaimed, "What, never been upset in a gig? What a slow fellow you are. You've never lived." He then immediately drove the wheels on one side of the gig up onto the bank of the road so that it fell over on its side and both men were thrown out.

On another occasion he was riding in his gig with a horsedealer. The gig was being pulled by two horses, one of which Jack was planning to buy from the dealer. He turned to the dealer and asked whether the horse was a good jumper and, without waiting for a response from the dealer, aimed both horses straight at the turnpike gate ahead of them. One of the pair jumped high over the gate but the second, the horse that belonged to the dealer, simply ran right into it. Inevitably the gig was turned over and both men were thrown out. History doesn't tell us what happened to the horses because of these escapades!

4. On leaving Pole Bank you return back towards the Shooting Box until, reaching a crossroads amongst the tracks you turn right.

The path to the left is signposted to Medlicott but the track you follow to the right (the east) has no signpost. This track soon brings you onto a tarmac road beside the Boiling Well where you turn left.

The Boiling Well has nothing to do with boiling water. The ground around here consists of very springy, soft turf which normally traps a great deal of air. At just this point, there is a spring. If you jump up and down on the turf just beside where the water emerges, you will push out the air trapped in the turf and it will bubble up in the spring, so that it appears to be boiling. It won't work, however, if the ground is too waterlogged with very little air trapped within in!

5. Leaving the Boiling Well, walk on a few yards before turning left onto a turf track once again. This is really a shortcut to avoid the vehicle route, which turns left further on and you soon rejoin the tarmac road for a short while. Again, you soon leave the tarmac road once more, this time to follow a track going north. This track has a National Trust sign by the entrance indicating that it is for "Authorised Vehicles Only". Follow this track for about a mile.

There is a new wire fence all along the right-hand side of the track at this point which was erected during the Foot and Mouth outbreak in 2001 and will probably be left here for some years to come. All the animals within this fenced area had to be slaughtered and it has since been restocked with sheep. It is hoped that, by keeping them within a fenced area, the new herd will eventually become hefted to their land. "Hefted" sheep are those which have learnt to know their own territory and therefore stay within boundaries that are otherwise unmarked. Thus, by the time the fencing deteriorates the flock will have come to know the limits of its territory and will not stray beyond it.

There are a few gates and stiles in the fencing and these lead down towards Church Stretton. A reminder of the ferocity of the weather in these hills is the fact that the old annual fair held in the town each November used to be known as the Dead Man's Fair. This was because so many people would get caught in bad weather conditions in the hills on their way home from the fair and perish.

6. Eventually the track meets up with a tarmac road where you turn right. Just before reaching the northern edge of the National Trust area with its cattle grid, you will notice a turning off to the left (beside a sign saying "No barbecues"). Follow this track which leads across a spring and through a gate into a field. The path is no longer so clearly marked so keep to the right-hand side to the far end of the field, across another ford into the next field, and so on through four fields altogether.

As you pass through the third of these fields you will see an old marker stone just on the other side of the fencing. It's an estate boundary marker and the metal plaque on the far side reads "Township of Batchcott, Manor of Cotharcott, TJ Powys Esqr, 1791". It's still being used today, as on the facing side there is a clearly carved trig sign.

7. When you reach *two* gates at the end of the fourth field, go through the gate on the right. It has a white painted arrow pointing ahead on the wooden gatepost.

For some time on this walk you have been following an ancient routeway, possibly some 3000 years old, called the Portway. It follows the length of the Long Mynd and was a safe route for travellers in dangerous times in the past. If you were a tradesman carrying all your goods and wealth with you as you wandered around the countryside from one market to the next, you would have felt much safer in a landscape with few trees – you could see other travellers from a long way off. The wooded valleys gave far too much cover for thieves.

At this point on the walk the Portway is quite well defined by the slight banks on either side of the track.

8. From now on the fence is on your left-hand side. Pass through two more gates and immediately after the second gate (which has a sign on it reminding you to shut the gate) there is a stile and footpath sign pointing to the left. The route now joins the Shropshire Way into the Golden Valley. Follow the path downhill. At the far end of the field, there is another stile just to the left of a holly tree. Continue downhill following the Shropshire Way markers, over a bridge made from two railway sleepers, towards Lower Darnford Farm.

Before reaching the farm, however, look for the signs for the footpath going to the right. This track goes through gates and over stiles all the way back to Ratlinghope. Finally it comes down to the Darnford Brook where there is a small concrete bridge leading to a lane between two farmhouses. This opens onto a road where, on turning to the right, you will see Ratlinghope church ahead of you.

The Golden Valley is a lovely name which is very apt if you walk along here in the autumn. But golden coloured leaves are unlikely to have any connection with the name. In all probability, it comes from the Welsh word "dwr" meaning water. When the French-speaking Norman invaders arrived here they would have heard this word and thought it sounded like the French "d'or" meaning golden, hence the name we have today.

Another name of interest here is the name Ratlinghope, meaning "the valley where Ratta's people live". It's not so much the meaning of the name but, rather, its pronunciation that catches people out – it's normally pronounced "Ratchup".

Ratlinghope church

Walk 14: Plaish

A judge who broke his word

Distance and time: 7 miles (11km); 3.5 hours.

Starting point: Beside the church in Church Preen. The lane to the church is just a gravel track and can be easily missed; there is a public footpath sign pointing along the lane with a sign attached to it which reads "To church only".

Maps: Landranger Map 137 or Explorer Map 217.

Terrain: The countryside here can best be described as "rolling hills" and the walk wanders up and down all the time. There are also numerous stiles (18 if they are all operational).

Refreshments and toilets: There are no facilities on the walk at all. The nearest pubs are the Royal Oak in Cardington and the Wenlock Edge Inn on the B4371 near Easthope.

Introduction

Soon after I came to live in Shropshire I read an article about the county in a national newspaper. It in, Shropshire was described as "that still cobwebbed country". It's a description that is particularly apt when used to describe the small little paths and lanes wending between the low hills and amongst the fields that this walk follows.

The Walk

Before starting on the walk make sure you first look inside the churchyard and find the enormous yew tree there. As they age they start to rot internally, so yew trees are notoriously difficult to age. This one, however, has a plaque beside it that tells everyone not only that it is the oldest tree in Europe (a debatable claim in view of the problems in dating) but also states that it was planted in "approx 457AD". I am always delighted by that approximation!

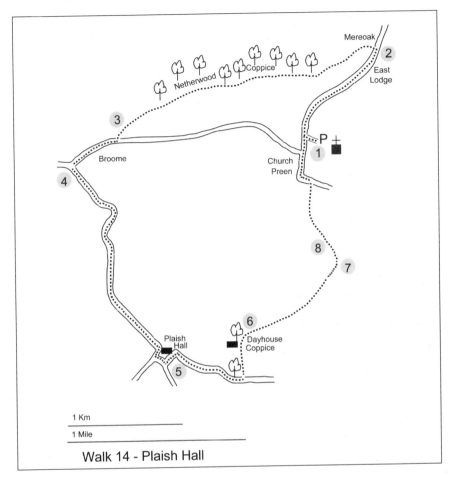

Walk 14 - Plaish Hall

1. Having visited the oldest tree in Europe start the walk by returning back up the gravel track to the tarmac country lane where you turn to the right.

2. After three-quarters of a mile, just beyond East Lodge house there is a farm entrance on the left with a footpath sign indicating the route of Ippikin's Way. The path leads across three fields and in the fourth it veers to the far right-hand corner after which it keeps along the edge of the fields with the woodland of Netherwood Coppice on the steep slope on your right. Follow Ippikin's Way for about a further one and a half miles until, just

beyond where the woodland ends the track leads you down the hill towards Broome Cottage.

The view from the point where you come past the forest is excellent, particularly looking towards the east where Ippikin, the highwayman, had his hideout amongst the caves below Wenlock Edge.

3. Broome Cottage is a private house and the public footpath goes through the drive onto the tarmac country lane beyond where you turn to the right.

As you walk along this stretch of road you will get a good view of the hill of Caer Caradoc ahead with the faint markings on it of an ancient hill fort. There are several hills in this part of the country that are called Caer Caradoc and each one is said by the people who live beside it to be the site of the great battle when Caractacus was defeated.

Caractacus is the Latin name for a British prince, Caradoc or Cradog. He lived, originally, in south-eastern Britain at the time of the Roman invasion in AD43 and, although his father yielded to the invading army, he refused to submit. He and his band of Celtic warriors fought as guerrillas for a number of years, but the Roman army steadily worked its way across Britannia, subduing the people as it went. Finally, the Romans decided that the only way in which to defeat Caractacus would be to force him into a full-scale battle. And that battle took place somewhere around Shropshire.

Caractacus was defeated but he managed to escape and fled to the north. However, it wasn't long before the Romans subdued the people there too and, as part of the peace treaty made with the northern Britons, Caractacus was handed over to the Romans.

He was taken to Rome where he was paraded, in his iron shackles, through the streets of the city. He should really have ended his days meeting some lions in the Colisseum. However, the Roman emperor was so impressed by the dignity with which this warrior met all the trials and indignities heaped upon him that he decided to spare Caractacus who spent the rest of his life living in relative peace in Rome.

Sadly, the story of Caractacus seldom features in modern history books, which is a pity because he is undoubtedly the earliest, properly documented, hero that our country can claim.

And where, exactly, did that battle take place? No-one knows for sure but modern historians tend to think that it was fought perhaps at the hill fort beside Llanymynech, or it might have been somewhere in the Breidden Hills.

4. At the next road junction turn left following the sign to Plaish which is one and a quarter miles away. On entering the village you soon come to the back of Plaish Hall, a magnificent 16th-century brick mansion. The route of the walk takes you all the way around the house, turning left at both of the two road junctions that you come to.

Plaish Hall (pronounced Plash) was built by Judge Leighton and it was while the house was being built that, one day, a man was tried for murder in the Judge's court and subsequently found guilty. It so happened that this man was a master bricklayer and the Judge offered him a pardon if the brickie would build him the finest of chimneys for his new mansion.

I think you will agree as you walk around the house that it does indeed have the most magnificent chimneys. However, when the chimneys were completed the Judge is said to have gone back on his word and hanged the murderer from one of his own chimneys. The house has been haunted by the bricklayer ever since.

Plaish Hall

Interestingly, when renovations were done on the house in 1916 a skeleton (complete with a noose around its neck) was found bricked up in one of the chimneys and subsequently buried in Cardington churchyard.

It is also said locally that the chimneys "bleed blood". However an analysis has been done on the liquid that oozes from the chimneys and it would appear that it's just rainwater that has been discoloured by the iron content in the bricks themselves. But we won't let a few facts destroy a good story!

5. Beyond Plaish Hall the lane turns to the right and goes down hill. At the bottom of the hill, there's a stream with a bridge over it and, just beyond, a stile into a field on the left. Follow the footpath along the edge of the field with the stream on your left until you come to a stile at the far end. This stile leads into the back of a private garden with a further stile immediately on the right leading uphill again through Dayhouse Coppice.

6. At the top of the hill there's another stile into a large field. It is difficult to see the route here as it clears the top of the hill – make your way diagonally across the field to the far right-hand corner. The next two fields are both reached over stiles and in each case the exit from the field is near to the far left-hand corner. You are walking towards the north-east in each case. This section of footpath is not often walked and can be somewhat overgrown with no clear path through the fields. If this is the case, it will be easiest to walk around the edge of the field.

7. On entering the third field, via a stile with a bridge made from two railway sleepers over a ditch, the direction of the footpath changes towards the north-west, in other words towards the far left-hand corner of the field.

8. The next field is entered over two stiles. This time head for the far right-hand corner where there is a gate and the beginnings of a well defined vehicle track which leads through a second gate onto the tarmac road into the village of Church Preen. Turn left to walk into the village. You will pass the graveyard on your left and then see the turning on your right for the track that leads back to the church itself.

Walk 15: Wenlock Edge

A story teller's haven

Distance and time: 5.5 miles (9km); 3 hours.

The short loop from the National Trust car park on the top of Wenlock Edge makes an ideal walk for very young children.

Starting point: Car park in Easthope Wood, OS reference 563959. Along the B4371, there is a cross roads with two minor roads leading to Lushcott to the west and Easthope to the east. Immediately on turning into the Lushcott road there is a dead-end lane signposted to Easthope Wood. The car park is on the left just before the road goes under an old iron railway bridge.

Maps: Landranger Map 138 or Explorer Map 217.

Terrain: This walk may be relatively short but there are a number of steep climbs up and down. Some sections can be very muddy after heavy rain. There are eight stiles.

Refreshments and toilets: The Wenlock Edge Inn is on the route and there are numerous pubs and coffee shops in Much Wenlock.

Useful contacts: Wenlock Edge Inn – 01746 785678

Introduction

Shropshire is a land of legends and stories and this tradition is alive and well in the 21st century, particularly at the Wenlock Edge Inn. Here you will find the oldest story-telling club in the country. The members meet each month to tell their tales or simply just to listen. Everyone is welcome.

The walk

Park in Easthope Wood car park.

1. The car park is right beside the disused railway line that used to link Much Wenlock with Craven Arms. Follow the line of the track northwards over the railway bridge. After half a mile, the track forks with a lane leading to the right, up the hill signposted

to Ippikin's Rock. A further sign, again to Ippikin's Rock, directs you to the right along a narrow footpath. At the top of the hill, over a stile, you will find a magnificent view looking towards Wales awaiting you.

I feel Ippikin's Rock should be called Ippikin's Lookout because if Ippikin, the thief, really existed that is how he would have used this rock. Ippikin was a robber living in early medieval times, if not even earlier. Some say he was an outlaw in Saxon times. Whenever he may have lived, he had a hideout in one of the caves along the rock face here from where he and his gang would attack the unwary traveller. One day, while all the men were in the cave gloating over the treasure that they had hidden there, there was a rockfall and the entrance to the cave was blocked, trapping Ippikin and his men inside. Ever since then, Ippikin has haunted the area.

Ippikin always wore a golden chain and, for those people who have sufficient imagination, the mark of it can be seen on this rock. But whatever you do, you must never stand on this spot and call out for the robber for if you should do so, it is said that he will appear and throw you down the cliff to your death.

After admiring the view turn around and you will see the Wenlock Edge Inn behind you to the east. This pub has become a centre for storytellers from all over the country who congregate here one evening each month to tell their stories. Anyone can join in, so go along. You will be especially welcome if you are prepared to tell a tale!

2.   From the viewpoint walk through the kissing gate, crossing over two fields to enter the car park for the Wenlock Edge Inn. If you are not stopping at the pub for a drink then turn to the right on reaching the main road (the B4371) and then immediately left down the lane signposted to Easthope and Brockton. Follow the lane to the village of Easthope where St Peter's churchyard is haunted by two monks.

These monks once lived in Easthope in the days when the manor belonged to the Priory at Much Wenlock. They were given some gold and began to fight over it until, eventually, they both tumbled down the stairs of the Manor into the cellar where they were found dead some time later. They were buried in the churchyard and can still sometimes be seen continuing their fight above their graves.

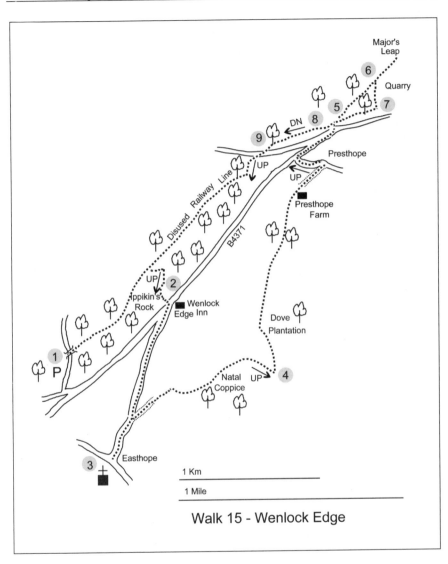

Major's
Leap

6

Quarry

5

7

DN 8

9 UP

UP

Presthope

UP

Disused Railway Line

Presthope
Farm

B4371

Dove
Plantation

UP
2

Ippikin's
Rock

Wenlock
Edge Inn

1
P

Natal UP 4
Coppice

3
Easthope

1 Km

1 Mile

Walk 15 - Wenlock Edge

The village and churchyard are both also haunted by William
Garmston who was murdered here in 1833. If you should go to live in
Easthope, it won't be long before you will be visited by William one
night. He occasionally wakes people up when he stands at the bottom
of their beds in order to have a look at the stranger who has just
arrived in his village.

The church at Easthope

3. Leave Easthope by walking back along the lane the way you came, but this time turn off right onto a track with a footpath sign for the Shropshire Way, which you will follow for the next two miles. The lane enters a field. Keep to the right-hand side of the field, turning right by the single tree and over a stile into another field just below Natal Coppice. On reaching the trees turn left, eventually crossing over the open field towards two tall oak trees at the other side of the field where you will turn right. There are regular Shropshire Way markers to keep you on the correct route. The path takes you over a stile into what appears to have once been an old sunken way which, judging by the amount of bird seed left here in winter, is now being used for the rearing of pheasants.

4. Emerging from the trees into an open field, turn left and walk along the edge of the field until you enter Dove Plantation. On leaving the plantation the footpath signs disappear – keep to the left of the field, heading towards a solitary oak tree and then follow the hedge line, keeping the hedge always on your left. At the far end of the field, by a stile, there is a Shropshire Way sign to confirm that you are on the route as you walk between two old hedge lines. A further stile brings you to an open field where the path leads towards a copse of trees.

Walk through the copse and continue in a straight line to the far side of the field where you bear right onto a track which is clearly defined. Follow the track until it reaches a tarmac road opposite Wenlock Fencing. Turn left, up the hill to the main road (the B4371). On reaching the main road turn right and walk towards Much Wenlock until you reach the National Trust Wenlock Edge car park.

This short stretch of road can be very busy and you may see a hitchhiker walking along. It would probably be wisest to ignore him if you see him – it could well be the ghost of a hitchhiker killed here in the 1960s who has been walking, and trying to hitch a lift, along this road ever since.

5.   This area of woodland is maintained by the National Trust and the route of the walk now includes a short loop, indicated on the display board in the car park as the Lime Kiln Walk. The path starts at the far right-hand corner of the car park, and is indicated by a red arrow on a waymarker post. At first, the path is gravelled but it soon forks and you take the left fork, off the gravelled path, following the sign towards Knowle Quarry.

6.   After one third of a mile the path reaches a T-junction. It's a good idea to follow the path to the left for a short distance because the views are magnificent and the feeling of being on top of the earth, with the steep cliffs to both left and right, is quite strange. Bear in mind, however, that you will have to return this way to continue the walk because your route should be to turn right following the red arrows for the Lime Kiln Walk.

This detour takes you to Major's Leap, named for Major Smallman who lived in nearby Wilderhope Manor during the Civil War in the 17th century. A Royalist soldier, Major Smallman was at home one day when a posse of Roundheads came to arrest him. He escaped on horseback, riding along the Edge towards Much Wenlock. The Roundheads chased after him and began to catch up so that Major Smallman realised he couldn't escape. And so, in a frantic bid to get away, he forced his horse to jump over the cliff somewhere near here. The horse was killed but the Major managed to grab the branch of a crab apple tree as he fell and survived.

The Roundheads weren't prepared to risk the lives of their horses by jumping off the cliff after him and so he managed to escape. Major Smallman died some years later but he is still around – he haunts Wilderhope Manor, which is now used as a Youth Hostel.

7. This section of the path has been laid out with display boards describing the recently restored 19th-century lime kilns that you pass and the local geology. Never mind the ghosts, you are now walking on rocks that were laid down over 400 million years ago. Follow the path all the way back to the Wenlock Edge car park.

8. On re-entering the car park go to the far side, near the main entrance where there is a track with a gate across it. Having walked around the gate, about 10 metres along the track there is a sign for two walks. Follow the sign to the left, towards "Easthope Wood ½ mile", which takes you down some steps along an old sunken trackway. After about 200 metres there is a further sign leading to Easthope Wood up some stairs to the left and onto a path that meanders through the forest and eventually reaches the road to Hughley, which you cross over. This area can be very muddy after heavy rain.

"The vane on Hughley steeple veers bright, a far-known sight." Although A.E. Housman published his book of poetry, 'The Shropshire Lad', over 100 years ago, visitors still regularly visit Hughley church to see the suicides' graves that he described in one of the poems. Actually, when Housman wrote this he was describing another church altogether because, as you can see from here, there is no spire on

Hughley's church. Apparently he just liked the sound of the name Hughley and thought it would work well for the poem when he wrote it!

9. Crossing over the road you enter Easthope Wood. You are now following the Jack Mytton Way, a bridle route. This leads you up a steep slope to reach the old, disused railway line where you turn right and follow the railway line and the Jack Mytton Way all the way back to the car park.

Walk 16: Much Wenlock
A beautiful saint

Distance and time: 6 miles (10km); 3 hours.

Starting point: Station Road, Much Wenlock.

Maps : Landranger Map 127 or Explorer Map 242.

Terrain: Country lanes and footpaths across fields in gently undulating countryside. There are six stiles.

Refreshments and toilets: None in the country section of the walk; numerous pubs and coffee shops in Much Wenlock.

Useful contacts: The Museum and Tourist Information Centre – 01952 727679; Much Wenlock Priory – 01952 727466

Introduction

The little town of Much Wenlock is easily one of the prettiest in Shropshire. It grew up around the early 7th-century monastery founded for St Milberga, which was subsequently to become an important Cluniac priory.

The Walk

Although marked on the town maps, the car park next to the Priory is for visitors to the Priory only. The walk therefore starts from Station Road where there is plenty of parking space.

1. Having parked your car walk up along Station Road and look out for the metal plaque on the pavement which reads "Wenlock Olympian Trail 1200". This is one of a series that commemorates William Penny Brooks, the 19th-century Wenlock doctor who began the Olympic movement here in Much Wenlock. About half-way between the plaque and the converted railway station there is a footpath leading across a field towards the Priory, which you follow.

    The present ruined priory was founded soon after the time of the

Norman Conquest by Roger de Montgomery. But, in fact, the first religious house on this site had been founded long before, in the 7th century by Prince Merewald of Mercia, a son of King Penda, especially for his daughter. It was a common practice in those days for the daughters of the nobility to run monasteries (both for men and women) and this was the case here. Milberga was to become the abbess of Much Wenlock and is now known as St Milberga.

Much Wenlock Priory ruins

There are a number of stories associated with the saint. She was a beautiful maiden, inevitably, and one day when out walking in the Corve Valley she was pursued by a lustful young man. Milberga fled from him, crossed over the River Corve and then fell to her knees to pray to God to rescue her from a fate worse than death. God did indeed come to her rescue because, just as the young man began to cross the river he sent a sudden torrent of water washing downstream which swept the young man away. In grateful thanks for the preservation of her virginity Milberga founded a church on the site where she had prayed – it's the ancient church that can still be seen at Stanton Lacy.

It would seem that this girl never learnt. On another occasion, she went out riding on her own in the Clee Hills. This time, however, she was pursued for two days and two nights by hunting dogs. Finally she got away from the dogs but, exhausted, she fell off her horse and would have died of thirst. But the horse kicked at the ground and, miraculously, a spring suddenly burst through the ground giving her water and saving her life so that she was able to make her way safely home. This happened in what is now the village of Stoke St Milborough where the spring can still be found.

2. Turn left in the Priory car park and follow the tarmac lane at the end of the car park for half a mile until it ends in front of Downs Mill. Follow the 'Shropshire Way' marker on the right-hand side of the gate along the gravel path track and on to the path to the right of the buildings. Go over a pair of stiles beside a stream, and then bear left until you reach the tarmac lane in front of Bradley Farm where you turn right.

3. You are now on a tarmac country lane which you follow for the next mile to Wyke. In Wyke, there are two junctions; at each one take the turning to the left.

4. After a further half a mile there is a gravel track leading off to the left. It is signposted as a public footpath route for the Shropshire Way. The track leads to Woodhouse Farm but just before the entrance to the house there is a path signposted to the left into a field. Notice that, on the maps, the footpath here goes across the field but the farmer has erected a sign directing walkers around the right-hand side of the field. Walk around the field and look out for the gap in the hedge on your right where you cross a small ditch and enter the next field through a metal gate.

5. Turn left and walk with the hedge now on your left. The route crosses a stile into a large field where the path goes straight on for about half the length of the field before crossing the field to the right. Head directly for the centre of the buildings of Bradley Farm and leave the field using the two stiles in the corner. Walk through the farmyard onto the tarmac lane and, this time, turn to your right.

6. Just before the lane meets the main road of the A4169 turn to the left. At first this appears to be the parking area behind a private house but at the far end there is a footpath sign directing you onto the disused railway back to Station Road. After walking for

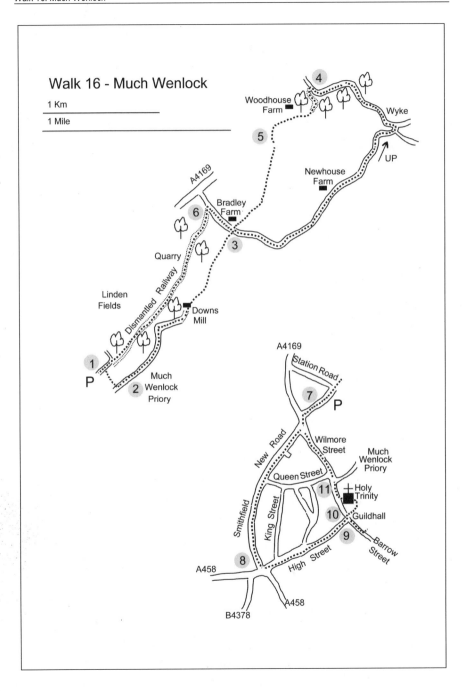

Walk 16 - Much Wenlock

1 Km

1 Mile

a mile, the route takes you between two embankments. There are three flights of stairs leading off to the right, take the third flight and you will find you are on a path overlooking the playing fields next to the school, the Linden Fields. Turn left and walk to Station Road.

7. This time walk to the bottom of Station Road and then cross the road at the end to walk along New Road and Smithfield.

At the end of Smithfield notice the old squatter's cottage on the left. Ancient law stipulated that if you could erect, overnight, a structure with a chimney and have a fire blazing in that chimney before morning you could claim the rights to the land. Squatters' cottages are often therefore easily identifiable by the fact that they have a large chimney which was built first and then, having established a claim to the site, the homeowner had time to add the cottage onto the chimney at a later date.

This particular cottage was once occupied by Nanny Morgan. She was a witch and lived here accompanied by live toads and, I am sure, the inevitable black cat. She possessed "the evil eye" and could cause bad luck to anyone who upset her. On the other hand, young girls used to come and visit her from far and near because, apparently, she was able to produce very effective love potions. These would ensure that those gentlemen who were a little slow in asking for a girl's hand could be rapidly brought to the altar!

8. At the end of Smithfield turn left and walk along High Street to the Guildhall at the T-junction at the far end.

Much Wenlock is an ancient town with numerous ghosts. Look out for the beautifully restored timber building on the left, opposite the Talbot Inn. It is haunted by two children wearing Victorian clothing who can often be seen playing with a spinning top on one of the balconies.

Further down the street you may wish to stop for a drink in the George and Dragon. If, while you are drinking here a large black dog approaches you, take care before you put your hand out to stroke it. It might just disappear.

The black dog was a fierce guard dog that belonged to a former landlord. No-one cared for it except for the landlord's daughter so that, ever since the dog died, it has come back regularly to look for the girl who fed it and gave it the love and affection it craved.

9. When you reach the road junction beside the clock turn to the right and walk 100 metres up Barrow Street until you see a small lane on the left leading to private houses. Walk down this lane and you will see a stone well on the right-hand side, dedicated to St Milberga. Then return the way you came, back to the clock and the Guildhall, which will now be on your right.

The Guildhall, Much Wenlock

Legend tells us that the Guildhall at the end of the High Street was built in two days. This seems astounding until you notice that it is largely timber framed. If all the timber was already on site, and there was a sufficient workforce available, erecting the frame of the building could well have taken only a couple of days. This was how such buildings would have been built from medieval times. Before continuing with the walk, look out for the two pairs of handcuffs attached to one of the posts in the front of the building.

The Guildhall is also haunted. The open area on the ground floor has been a market place for many centuries and there are often markets held there now. If you see some people huddled in a corner who look a bit strangely dressed, they might just be ancient ghosts.

10. Continue the walk by passing through the walkway under the Guildhall into the churchyard beyond where you turn to the left. Walk around the church and, to the south of the chancel, you will find the grave of Dr William Penny Brooks.

William Penny Brooks was born in Much Wenlock and was a doctor here from the mid 1800s. He had the very novel idea, for the time, that fresh air and exercise would be good for his patients. To this end, in 1850, he began the "Wenlock Games". At first, this was a very casual affair with local people taking part in various races and, if they were lucky, winning a packet of tea.

But the games grew in popularity so that within 20 years people were coming to the Games from far and near and the quality of the races and the variety of the events increased accordingly. Word spread so that, eventually, in 1890 Baron de Coubertin visited Much Wenlock from France and he was so impressed that he then organised the first international Olympic Games. To this day, the Wenlock Games are still held annually with, often, a representative from the International Olympic Committee attending!

11. Walk back to the main street and turn right to pass the Bull Ring and walk along Wilmore Street to return to Station Road.

Walk 17: Ironbridge

Two murders and a bridge

Distance and time: 5 miles (8km); 2.5 hours.

Starting point: Car park beside the Iron Bridge on the southern bank. Please note that this is a Pay and Display car park.

Maps: Landranger Map 127 or Explorer Map 242.

Terrain: Generally quite easy with one steep slope. However, the last part of the walk follows part of the Severn Way and is on land that is liable to flooding. This means that, although the path is regularly maintained, occasionally sections of the path can slip into the river; this is particularly the case along the narrow path opposite the power station. There are three stiles.

Refreshments and toilets: There are numerous pubs and coffee shops in Ironbridge.

Useful contacts: Ironbridge Tourist Information Centre – 01952 432166; Ironbridge Gorge Museum Trust – 01952 433522; Buildwas Abbey – 01952 433274. (Please note that Buildwas Abbey is only open to the public in the summer.)

Introduction

Although we think of Ironbridge as the product of the Industrial Revolution in the 18th century there has always been industry here. Even in medieval times, much of the income of Buildwas Abbey was derived from iron industries. With the development of industry here in the 1700s strangers coming to the area from that time often saw Ironbridge as the "very gates of hell" with the sulphurous smell that pervaded the whole place, the noise of the constantly working furnaces and the black, sooty dirt and grime that covered everything.

The walk

Before starting the walk take time to admire the Iron Bridge which was built in 1779. It was a toll bridge and the toll house is just beside the car park, with a list of the tolls payable on the outside wall.

The Iron Bridge

The Iron Bridge was built by Abraham Darby III. He was a Quaker and it is part of the Quaker belief that they should not have their likeness portrayed in paintings or on statues. However, for those with sharp eyes, it is said that there is a portrait of Abraham Darby actually on the bridge. Look carefully and the outline of the frame below the centre of the bridge and you may be able to make out the shape of a man's profile – I wonder if Abraham Darby truly did look like this?

1. Start the walk along the disused railway track to the left of the toll house. There is also a tarmac road parallel to it and between it and the river, but choose the railway track that immediately goes under a brick bridge. Walk right to the end of the track, just in front of one of the cooling towers for the Buildwas Power Station.

2. Beside the gate on the left there is a 'V' shaped stile. Pass through this and turn right on to the footpath that follows the Shropshire Way marker. The path rises quite steeply and soon meets a side track where you turn right, this time following a yellow arrow

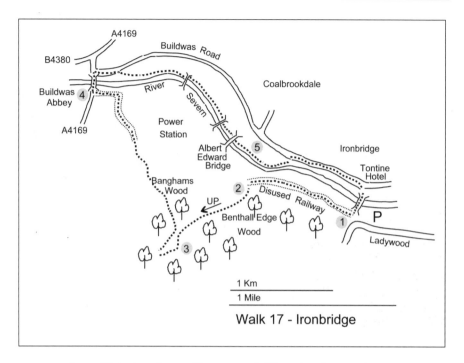

Walk 17 - Ironbridge

marker. This track continues uphill, soon becoming a narrow path along the right-hand edge of the forest and overlooking the power station.

From here you will have an excellent view of the Severn valley with the ruins of Buildwas Abbey in the distance and the Wrekin beyond. Geologists will tell you that the Wrekin is made of volcanic rock and is, in fact, the oldest rock in Shropshire. Local people, however, know different.

There was once a giant who fell out with the people who lived in the town of Shrewsbury and, as revenge against them, this giant decided he would destroy the town. He piled a huge lump of earth on his spade and walked across the country towards Shrewsbury with the intention of dropping this earth on the town and obliterating it. In the course of his walk, however, he met a cobbler and the two of them fell into conversation.

The cobbler was appalled when he realised the giant's plans, particularly since it would have meant the loss of so many of his customers. He therefore showed the giant his bag of damaged boots and shoes that he was carrying to his home to repair.

"Look," he said to the giant, "Shrewsbury is such a long way from here that I have worn out all these boots and shoes just by walking all that distance."

The giant was amazed to realise that Shrewsbury was so far away and promptly decided that it would be too much trouble for him to walk so far and, instead, he dropped the lump of earth where he was. And so the Wrekin was formed.

3. Eventually, the path flattens out just before a junction where several paths and tracks meet. You follow the well-defined track to the right, taking a hair-pin bend to walk downhill back towards, and then past, the power station. At one point, the track forks but there is a wooden sign nailed to a tree between the fork indicating that the footpath goes to the right.

Eventually you enter a permanent caravan park through a gate; walk straight through the park along the tarmac road keeping the permanent chalets on your left. This lane leads to the A4169 Telford to Much Wenlock road where you turn right.

Just before you reach the main road, you will be walking parallel to a railway line where you may notice that there are a number of wagons loaded with coal – these are to supply the power station, which is coal-fired.

If you wish to visit Buildwas Abbey you will see a little path across the road which is a short cut (unsignposted) to the Abbey car park. Buildwas Abbey was a Cistercian monastery founded in the 12th century. Like so many, it was dissolved by Henry VIII in the 1500s and is now a ruin maintained by English Heritage.

Being the abbot of Buildwas Abbey would appear to have not been without its risks. In 1350 the Welsh were raiding in Shropshire and carried off the Abbot of Buildwas for ransom.

Another Abbot was murdered by one of the monks, a man called Thomas Tonge. Tonge fled into Wales but then found that life on the run was considerably harder than life had been in the monastery, so he decided that he wanted to go back. He returned to Buildwas, said how sorry he was for the murder he had committed and asked to be forgiven. Of course, good Christians should always forgive those who truly repent their sins. And so the monks at the Abbey were obliged to show Christian forgiveness and let him return.

I hope those monks who shared the dormitory with the repentant Tonge after his return slept easily in their beds!

4. To continue the walk, cross over the Buildwas Bridge and immediately turn right along the road at the other side of the bridge, towards Ironbridge once again. After about 200 metres you will come to a gate on the right-hand side with a sign for the Telford Angling Association on it and a stile beside it. Cross over the stile into the field and you will now be following the Severn Way all the way back to the Iron Bridge passing under three other bridges (opposite the power station) on your way.

One of these bridges, the Albert Edward Bridge, built in 1863, is named for the Prince of Wales who was to become King Edward VII. Victoria had always intended that he should be known as King Albert after her beloved husband but King Edward, always at loggerheads with his parents, had no intention of using that name when he acceded to the crown.

5. The Severn Way passes by the Ironbridge Rowing Club and enters the Riverside Park. Follow the path as far as you can along the river bank until eventually, just beyond the Museum of the River, you have to leave it to walk along the pavement beside the road to return to the Iron Bridge.

This stretch of pavement can often be flooded when the river is at its highest. If you have the chance to visit the Museum of the River look out for the markers for flood levels. Looking at the building from the outside you must try to imagine the water level for the worst flood (which occurred in 1795) reaching almost to the tops of some of the windows.

The River Severn can be treacherous with many dangerous currents and yet it was here that Matthew Webb learnt to swim – he was later to earn fame by becoming the first person to swim across the English Channel in 1875. Even as a young boy, at the age of eight, he

The Tontine Hotel, Ironbridge

saved one of his brothers from drowning in the river. Sadly, however, that was to be his own eventual fate.

Eight years after his Channel swim he tried to swim across the Niagara Rapids. He very soon got into difficulties. His body was recovered some miles downstream four days later and he was buried at Oakwood Cemetery, near Niagara Falls.

Before you walk over the bridge to return to the car park notice the Tontine Hotel. When the Iron Bridge was first built people came from far and near to see this amazing structure and this hotel was built to house the many visitors.

One visitor to the hotel some years later, however, was a local man. He had just murdered his landlady in nearby Ketley and was on the run. He was hiding out in room number five at the hotel when he was eventually cornered and arrested. From here, he was taken to Shrewsbury for his trial and, on being found guilty, he was eventually executed at Shrewsbury Prison. He was one of the last men to be hung for murder in the county. He still haunts the room where he was arrested, turning lights on and off and making clocks in the room run backwards.

Walk 18: Bridgnorth
The sad tale of two children

Distance and time: 6.5 miles (11km); over 3 hours.

Starting point: The station for the Severn Valley Railway. There is parking in the car park there although this will sometimes be very busy.

Maps: Landranger Map 138 or Explorer Map 218.

Terrain: Very easy walking. However, after wet weather (or floods) the path along the river bank can be very muddy and slippery. It can also become quite overgrown by the end of the summer season. There are 11 stiles.

Refreshments and toilets: There is a pub, the Unicorn Inn, at Hampton. If time is available, however, it is possible to take the ferry across the river to Hampton Loade where there are additional pubs.

Please note that this walk is not circular and you will therefore need to return to Bridgnorth on the Severn Valley Railway. The railway does not run a regular service (in the winter it is only a weekend service) and so train times should be checked before you set off.

Useful contacts: Bridgnorth Tourist Information Centre – 01746 763257; Severn Valley Railway – 01299 403816; Hampton Loade Ferry – 07966 183728

Introduction
Bridgnorth is a comparatively new town – it was only founded in AD1101! But there were certainly people living here long before there was a town – the caves in the sandstone rock on which the town perches would have made safe, cosy houses high above the river from the earliest times.

The walk
The walk starts from the entrance to the railway station building in Bridgnorth.

1. Facing the station entrance there is a footbridge that connects the station with the town. Use the footbridge to cross the valley

and, when you reach the road at the other side, look to your right and you will see, almost straight ahead, a path leading up the hill – Cannon Steps. Follow this path which brings you out at the top of the castle.

At this point you will find yourself at a magnificent viewpoint right at the southern end of the hill occupied by the town of Bridgnorth. The Cannon Steps are so-called because there used to be a cannon here that had been captured at the Battle of Sebastopol during the Crimean War. For 100 years, it guarded the town until, during the Second World War it disappeared. Iron pots and pans, iron railings and iron cannons were being collected from all over the country to provide the iron required to build Spitfires and Hurricanes. Unfortunately much of this iron was far too poor a quality to be risked in the building of planes and was used for other things entirely.

There's a Bridgnorth legend that states that the old cannon from here ended up under the streets of New York. It will have been shipped there as ballast in one of the ships returning to the USA that had previously been weighed down with tanks and armaments when it crossed the Atlantic to come to England.

2.   Just opposite the viewpoint you will see the entrance into the Castle Gardens. Walk through the gardens towards the Castle. (If, however, you are walking with a dog you will have to turn to the right at the top of Cannon Steps to walk along the Castle Hill Walkway as dogs are not allowed in the gardens.)

The first castle on this site was probably built in Saxon times but the ruined keep that you see leaning at an alarming angle ahead of you is all that remains of a much later Norman castle. The castle was once the stronghold of a man called Robert de Belesme, a particularly ghastly character. He was the eldest son of Roger de Montgomery. Roger had come over to England with William the Conqueror and been put in charge of all the territory now encompassed largely by the county of Shropshire. Some years later, in 1098, Robert inherited his father's English estates and was soon feared by all those who had any dealings with him.

Times were hard and leaders were expected to be ruthless but Robert's ruthlessness was extreme and he became a byword even for those times. Like many tyrants, both before and since, he not only

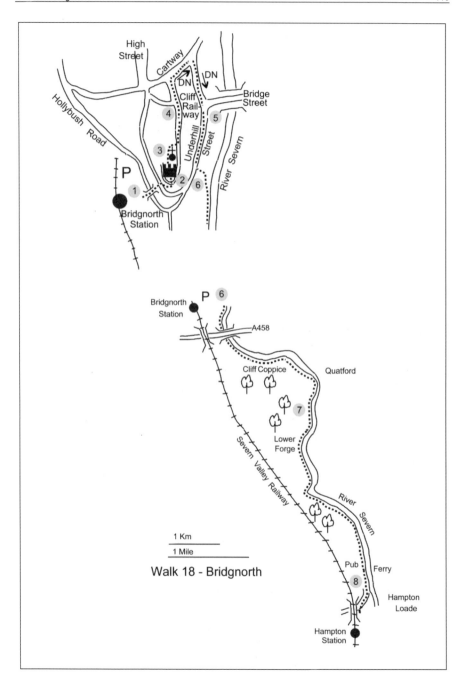

Walk 18 - Bridgnorth

1 Km

1 Mile

employed torturers but enjoyed torturing his victims himself. He is known to have once personally gouged out the eyes of a young boy whom he was holding as a hostage when the boy's father fell down on his word. On another occasion 300 of his prisoners were left to starve to death – apparently Robert de Belesme's reason for this was that it was Lent and they shouldn't therefore have had food anyway!

The ruined keep of Bridgnorth Castle

3. Walk to the right of the castle – if you dare. It's unlikely to fall on you as it has been leaning at just this angle (greater than that of the Leaning Tower of Pisa, in fact) ever since the keep was blown up after it was captured during the Civil War over 300 years ago. Beyond the castle you will see the church of St Mary Magdalene. Walk around the church, passing the main entrance, and bear to the right so that you reach the Castle Hill Walkway overlooking the Severn Valley. Here you turn to the left to walk towards the town.

Before continuing with the walk look across the valley towards the hills at the other side. You may be able to make out the outcrops of sandstone that appear all along these hills. The sandstone is extremely soft and, from time immemorial, people have carved out houses within the stone. Legend has it that one of the caves cut into the hills at the other side of the valley was occupied by one of King Alfred's grandsons. This man, who was called Ethelred, lived as a hermit in a cave that is known as the Hermitage to this day.

4. At the end of Castle Hill Walkway you will come to the cliff railway. Those of you who want to cheat can do so by using the railway to go to the bottom of the hill. The railway is the only surviving inland cliff railway in the country; it also has both the steepest and the shortest incline of any cliff railway in Britain.

Those of you who wish to continue the walk should go straight on, past the entrance to the cliff railway and along a pedestrian street just ahead, Castle Terrace. At the far end of Castle Terrace, you will see a shop (Natural Things) which is on Cartway. Turn right on Cartway and walk all the way down the hill, passing the Black Boy pub on the way. Bear in mind that this was once the main road leading into the town.

Just as you come to the bottom of the Cartway you will see ahead of you the Bassa Villa Bar and Grill in an old timber-framed house that dates from the 16th century. You are now in Low Town. Bridgnorth is divided between High Town around the castle on the top of the hill where the main market once was, and Low Town, the port area where all the goods coming into that market would have been landed. The Bassa Villa revives an old name for the district, it comes from Latin meaning the "basin of the town".

If you look into the garden of the Bassa Villa you may see what remains of the statues of two young children. They were produced to commemorate two children who have haunted the building ever since their deaths some time soon after the house was built. You're right down beside the River Severn here, a river that is notorious for its floods. Throughout history those people who chose to live in Low Town did so because they needed to live close to where the boats docked and they then had to live with the constant threat of floods.

It so happened that the two children who lived in this building were one day playing a game of hide and seek and went to hide in the cellar. While they were playing the townspeople were advised of an impending flood and, unaware that the children were still inside the building, their parents locked the house and the cellar while they went to take refuge on higher ground. After the floodwaters had receded, they came back to the house only to find that the two young children had been trapped and had drowned in the muddy waters. It's not just the children that haunt the building – their mother, now known as the Black Lady, can often be seen also as she searches for them.

5. You emerge from the Cartway onto the main road which leads to the bridge on your left. Cross over the road and walk straight ahead along Underhill Street, keeping the River Severn on your left – do not cross over the river.

If you have come down the hill on the cliff railway you will come out onto Underhill Street. Cross over the road and turn to the right.

As you walk along this road you will see several caves cut into the hill below the castle. Some of these were once occupied as houses, some served as cellars and stores. In fact, it's said that the even temperature of the caves was particularly good for storing ale, giving Bridgnorth an excellent reputation for the quality of its beer.

It was also the caves here that were to lead to the downfall of the castle during the Civil War. The castle was occupied by Royalist forces when the Parliamentarians attacked the town. The bombardment from both sides was severe – at one time a lucky (?) shot from the castle hit St Leonard's church at the northern end of the town which was being used as an arsenal. The church was blown up and the subsequent fire set much of High Town alight.

There was no way that the Parliamentarians were going to be able to take the castle by military force and so they came up with an excellent ruse. They decided to dig a tunnel underneath the castle, fill it full of dynamite and blow the whole hillside up! The tunnel was dug – it's over 20 metres long. Fortunately for the inhabitants of the castle, they were warned about what was being planned and given the option to surrender, which they wisely did. And so, the castle alone was blown up when charges were placed within the building, rather than the entire hillside.

6. Walk along Underhill Road until you reach an office block called Lasyard House. Just beyond Lasyard House there is a track leading off to the left, which takes you down to the river bank. At the end of the track you turn to the right and, from here until you reach Hampton, you are following the Severn Way downstream, with the river always just on your left. At first the path is very narrow and goes over a stile and through a field, passing under the Bridgnorth bypass.

From here to Hampton the path is clearly defined and used by a great many people. Some parts are quite narrow, however, and after rain (or, indeed, flood) the path can often become slippery and care needs to be taken. Moreover, at the end of each summer there are sections that become decidedly overgrown.

The River Severn is the longest river in Great Britain, some 210 miles (337km). Ever since the first people came and lived along its banks it served not only as an important source of food and water but also has been a vital means of communications. Traders have used the river but so, too, have plundering armies. The Vikings, for example, could travel far inland in their longboats and are known to have wintered one year somewhere on the banks of the Severn near here.

As you walk along by the river you will, after about two miles, see the little village of Quatford across the water. On the hillside above Quatford there is an ancient oak tree that, legend tells us, was already growing over a thousand years ago. It was soon after the Norman conquest and King William had just given Roger de Montgomery control of these lands. Roger sent back to France for his wife, Adelisa, to join him. As Adelisa crossed the English Channel, the ship on which she was travelling was caught in a terrible storm and, fearful for her life, Adelisa prayed to God to save them all. She vowed that, if her life should be spared and she could reach her husband, she would build a church on the spot where they met.

Roger was out hunting when Adelisa arrived in the area and, so the story tells us, the two met under this very oak tree. Certainly it's an extremely old oak tree; even its branches need to be propped up with wooden stakes. But would it have been old enough then for two people to have met underneath it's branches? I don't know. Incidentally, Adelisa fulfilled her vow, and built a church nearby.

7. You follow the Severn Way for a distance of just over five miles, always walking downstream and keeping the river on your left. When you see ahead of you a bridge that crosses the river to the pumping station you will know that you are nearly at Hampton – the blue arches of the bridge are actually large water pipes. The footpath enters Hampton through a camp site. Keep on the footpath next to the river until, after crossing over a stile, you will find the Hampton Loade ferry just beside you.

8. Just beyond the ferry you will find you are walking on a tarmac lane. It is here that you leave the Severn Way and continue walking along the tarmac towards the railway station which is on your left, just before you reach the railway bridge. To catch the train back to Bridgnorth you need to cross to the other side of the line.

Finally, as you leave the railway station back at Bridgnorth, spare a thought for the ghost who haunts the Holyhead Inn across the road. Presumably, he is a former landlord of the pub because he was once seen behind the counter, but nobody knows for sure. Sometimes he can be seen walking through a wall where once there was a doorway. Sometimes he can be heard upstairs, apparently switching the lights on and off – or, at least, that is what it sounds like.

Hampton station

Walk 19: Hopton Castle

"Remember Hopton!"

Distance and time: 4.5 miles (7km); 2.5 hours.

Starting point: The village of Hopton. There are no proper car parks in the village so please park with due care and consideration for those who live here.

Maps: Landranger Map 137 or Explorer Map 201.

Terrain: Although a short walk in terms of distance, there is a steep climb through the forest near the beginning of the walk. There are no stiles; however, there is one gate that cannot be moved and needs to be climbed over with care.

Refreshments and toilets: None on the walk, nor in the village of Hopton. The nearest pub is the Hundred House Inn at Purslow.

Introduction

No-one who watches news bulletins on the television can ever be unaware that there is no war worse that a civil war for its ferocity and sheer cruelty. Sadly, this was also the case with our own Civil War in the 17th century. The most ghastly act of that war took place in this peaceful countryside. At least I hope it was the most ghastly – I hate to think that there could have been worse atrocities.

The walk

Please note that Hopton Castle is on private land and is not open to the public. However, it can be easily seen from the road.

1. Walk to the far end (the western end) of the village, passing over the small bridge by the entrance to the church. Beyond the houses on the left, turn to the left into a field – there is a clearly marked track going through the field and a blue arrow on the gate post to confirm the route exists. Walk through three fields, following the track all the way until you enter woodland passing through the fourth gate on the track.

2. Once in the forest follow the earthen track as it first turns to the left and then, before you have gone 100 metres it meets a gravelled track where you turn to the right. As you walk along the gravel track, you pass an old quarry area and then, just as the track starts to go gently downhill look out for a footpath sign directing you to the left. This is a woodland path, indicated by a post with a red triangular arrow cut into it. The path is very steep and is also used by riders on mountain bikes so do listen out for them as they will be moving very fast.

3. You walk up this path, climbing all the time, for over half a mile until you come to a point where five paths meet. This junction also has a marker post with the number "9" and green arrows painted on it. Looking at the junction as though it were a roundabout you take the second exit, to walk along the gravel track to your left. Follow this gravel track for about one mile, passing numbered posts that seem to have no rhyme nor reason to them – number 8, then number 22, then number 23, until you reach number 26.

4. The post with number 26 sits beside a junction where one path goes straight on and another hairpins sharply to the right – follow the path to the right. Again you follow numbered posts – this time they are numbered consecutively and you walk past posts 34 and 33 until, when you reach post 32 you leave the gravel track to turn left onto an earth track.

5. As you walk through the forest at this point you will see fields just beyond the trees on your right – you are now walking along the edge of the forest. When you reach the next numbered post, number 31, the main track bears to the left but you keep straight on with the forest boundary always just on your right. After about 50 metres, you will see a wooden gate in the hedge line on your right. This gate cannot be moved at all and must be climbed over. There are no signs to confirm that this is the route of the path. However, as a concession to walkers, the barbed wire that exists along the hedge has been cut away from the gate itself! Once in the field turn to your left and continue walking down-

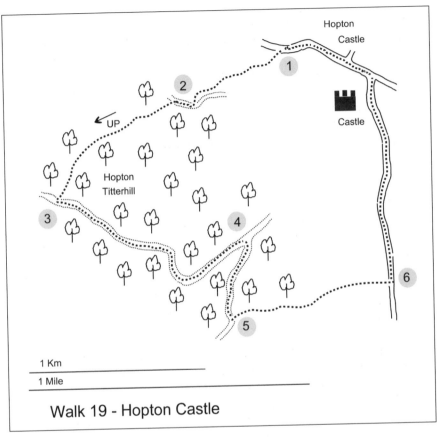

Walk 19 - Hopton Castle

hill, passing through a second field beyond which you reach the tarmac road.

6. This lane leads you directly to the village of Hopton. As you enter the village, you come to a T-junction in front of a recently restored timber-framed cottage where you turn to the left to walk towards the church.

As you walk towards the village you pass one house on your left and then, just before you reach the village itself, you will see the ruins of Hopton Castle in a field on your left. On a sunny day, it looks a beautiful spot and it is difficult to imagine the horrors that once took place here just before the castle was "so far demolished as to render it incapable for further defence".

Near the village of Hopton – all peaceful now!

It all happened during the Civil War in 1644. The castle was held for the Parliamentarian forces by 30 soldiers under the command of Samuel More. The Royalist army laid siege to the castle and tried to storm it on several occasions but were forced back each time. Because of this and the constant bombardment of the Royalists from the cannons within the castle, that small garrison of 30 men killed over 200 attackers.

Perhaps it is therefore no wonder that, when the castle garrison finally surrendered, the Royalists were in no mood to be lenient. The surrendering soldiers expected to be imprisoned but, instead, the revenge meted out to them by the Royalists has caused revulsion ever since.

There were two young maids in the castle who were stripped and beaten before being allowed to go. As for the men, however, they were just butchered. Limbs were cut off and the mutilated men were then herded into a pit. As they tried to climb out they were clubbed until eventually they were all horribly put to death.

One man, Major Phillips, offered £20 in order to have his life spared. £20 in those days would have been an enormous sum of money. His offer was readily accepted; he was taken into the castle to pay the money – and then he was stabbed to death.

We know exactly what happened here because the garrison's commander, Samuel More, was forced to watch as his men were so brutally murdered. He was then marched off to imprisonment in Ludlow Castle where he later wrote an account of the events that took place at Hopton.

As far as the Royalists were concerned, the surrender of Hopton Castle was cause for celebration. It is said that the bell ringers at Ludlow were given 1s 6d (7½p) to pay for drink when they rang the church bells to announce the news.

But, inevitably, word of the atrocity got out. Men had surrendered in good faith and then been horribly killed. Would it ever again be wise for Parliamentarians to accept the word of the Royalists? The story of all that happened here did the Royalist cause no good whatsoever and, in fact, for years afterwards whenever a Royalist gave his word on any subject whatsoever to a Parliamentary man, the standard response was, "Remember Hopton".

Is it any wonder that this site has been haunted by those men ever since?

Walk 20: Ludlow

A pub full of ghosts

Distance and time: 4.5 miles (7km); 3 hours.

Starting point: Car park off Upper Galdeford Road. Please note that this is a Pay and Display car park.

Maps: Landranger Map 137 or Explorer Map 203.

Please note that, although the walk follows some of the route of the Mortimer Trail, the route indicated on the OS maps is *not* the same as the one indicated on the ground by waymarkers. The walk outlined here follows the waymarkers on the ground.

Terrain: A steady climb after the Dinham Bridge but generally very easy walking; the bridleway can get boggy after heavy rain. There are two stiles and one gate that must be climbed.

Refreshments and toilets: None on the walk; plenty in Ludlow.

Useful contacts: Ludlow Tourist Information Centre – 01584 875053

Introduction

A planned town dating from Norman times, Ludlow was dominated by the Mortimer family through much of the Middle Ages and their influence is felt to this day. The town developed as an important local market adjacent to the castle and was, for a time in the 16th and 17th centuries, the virtual capital of all of the Welsh Marches and Wales.

The walk

Start from the car park off Upper Galdeford Road.

1. Walk to the main entrance of the car park at the top of the hill and then turn right to walk along the pedestrianised Tower Street. Turn to the right when you reach the main road to walk down Corve Street towards the Feathers Hotel. Walk across the street and into the courtyard of the Bull Inn.

Ludlow Castle

The Feathers Hotel must be one of the most beautiful in England with its fabulously decorated façade and was built in the early 17th century. But no-one knows who or what it is that haunts room number 211. People who have stayed in this room have often felt the air around them go suddenly cold and icy fingers touching them. One couple staying in the room were getting ready for bed when "something" pulled open the wardrobe doors. Other people have referred to clapping noises and footsteps hurrying by but, on investigating the noise, no reason for it has been found.

The Bull Inn across the road is far older than the Feathers. While restoration was being carried out some years ago a priest hole was discovered which, perhaps, explains the identity of the man who haunts the pub. Footsteps have often been heard in parts of the building that are empty and the ghost seems to make a habit, particularly, of checking on new landlords that come to run the pub. Perhaps, if he was hiding here in times of persecution and was nervous of being found, he might have good reason to want to check on the trustworthiness of new occupants!

2.   At the far end of the Bull Inn courtyard use the short flight of stairs leading into the churchyard beyond. Walk to the far end of the churchyard to College Street and turn left. Walk through the open Butter Market to the top of Broad Street and then turn right along Market Street. This is a pedestrian street parallel to, and on the far side of, the vehicular High Street. Walk along Market Street, passing the Globe Inn along the way.

The Globe Inn is haunted by an old man who wanders around the top floor dressed in his night attire – a long white night-shirt and night cap. He is seen carrying a candle but, somehow, the flame from the candle never flickers, even as he moves along.

3. On entering the open area of Castle Square, walk along the left-hand side of the Square passing the Tourist Information Centre until you reach Mill Street beyond. A little way down Mill Street you will see the Blue Boar pub on the right.

Can there be a pub in all of England that hosts more individual ghosts than this one? In fact, the present landlord and his family where so upset by the ghosts that, three months or so after arriving here, they were on the verge of leaving. They have stayed, however, and are now becoming accustomed to the other occupants of the building. And who are all these ghosts?

There's a 17th-century cavalier who is sometimes seen in broad daylight walking the length of the building from the front door to the rear. He's often seen by large groups of people and it's thought that he is the ghost responsible for tugging at the sleeves of ladies who sit on their own by the window. One lady recently became so upset by this constant touching that, despite reassurances that it was only a ghost, finally walked out of the building.

This ghost has now been given the name of George and is also always blamed when the taps for the casks in the cellar mysteriously turn themselves off.

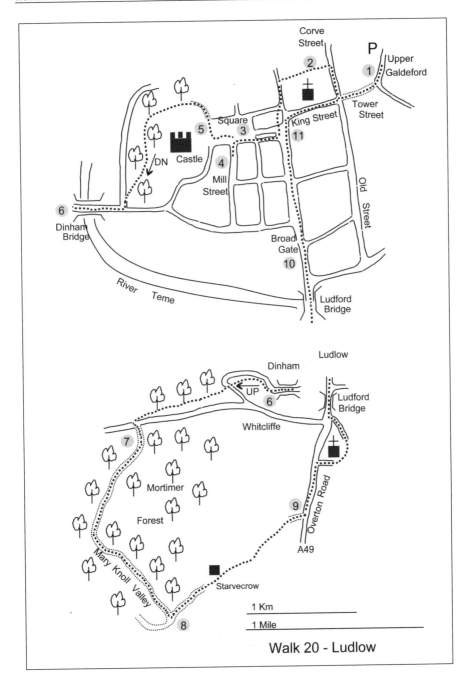

Walk 20 - Ludlow

There is also a ghost who leaves money (always old pennies, never new!) on the counter in the bar. Has someone remembered, better late than never, to pay for his drink?

The pub provides accommodation for visitors and many of them have seen the lady who walks along the corridor on the first floor. She was a teacher who lodged here in the 1830s and always looks very real to those who see her, until they realise that there's something wrong about the fixed, glazed expression on her face.

One of the rooms on the floor above is occupied by the ghost of an elderly man who is seen sitting on a stool, holding a clay pipe in his hands and sobbing his heart out. This room is always extremely cold. It makes no difference whether it's the middle of a hot summer or winter with all the heating on – guests who stay in this room always ask for an extra blanket. It was in this room sometime in the 18th century that a young girl who became pregnant out of wedlock committed suicide. Many people think that the sobbing man is her father.

But that's not the end of it. There are weird noises that can't be explained. Keys disappear only to be found much later in strange places. Even, recently, the landlord's son watched horrified as some unseen presence picked up his mobile phone and threw it across the room.

4. Return up Mill Street to the Square and, on turning left, you will see you are standing beside Castle Lodge.

Castle Lodge, on the corner between Mill Street and the market square, dates from the 1590s. Before this date, the building on this site was used as a prison for people from all over the region who were brought to have their cases tried at Ludlow's court. It was once described as "such a place of punishment that the common people call it a hell". The man who haunts the building is dressed in the costume of the Tudor period and is therefore thought to be not a prisoner, but the Sergeant who probably ran the prison.

5. Walk towards the Castle and just before the entrance follow the footpath to the right. This is the start of the Mortimer Trail, which you will follow for the next two miles. The trail goes all the way to Kington. The path winds around the hill and forks

The keep of Ludlow Castle

twice, take the right-hand fork each time, and leave the forest below the Castle on the Linney, opposite Mr Underhill's Restaurant. Turn left and then right to cross over the Dinham Bridge crossing the River Teme.

The castle ruins tower above the footpath and it is not difficult to imagine poor Marion de Bruyere who jumped to her death somewhere near here. Marion lived in the castle in the late 12th century. She had a secret lover and, late at night, Marion would often let him into the castle via one of the postern gates. He came regularly and no-one knew. Then one night, Marion went to the gate to meet her lover – only to discover that he had been using her merely as a means of entering the castle for, on this occasion, he was waiting for her with a group of armed men, all of them intent on taking the castle. Appalled by the way in which she had been tricked into betraying the castle, Marion grabbed her lover's sword and promptly killed him with it before fleeing to the castle's battlements from where she jumped to her death. Poor Marion has haunted the castle ever since.

6. Immediately after crossing the bridge you enter Whitcliffe Common to the left and then climb the steps ahead, following the Permissive Route/Mortimer Trail signs. The old quarry on the right was used for stone when the castle was built and the trail goes above it to the top of the cliff giving wonderful views back towards the castle through the trees.

When the path comes to a tarmac road, turn right. The road then hairpins back downhill towards Ludlow but your route goes straight on at this point along Lower Warburton Road. About 100 metres along the road a signpost for the Mortimer Trail is seen indicating a climb up the hill to the left. There are a number of footpaths in the forest but the trail is well marked. Follow the signs until you reach the main road linking Ludlow and Wigmore. Cross the road and enter the Mortimer Forest Country Park.

7. The Mortimer Trail is clearly marked through the forest. Although there are many trails marked out here, this is the main one. Note that the waymarkers on the ground do NOT coincide with the route that is marked on the Ordnance Survey maps. Follow the markers on the ground, walking first south-west and then turning towards the south-east above Mary Knoll Valley.

All the best legends are those based on fact and so it is with the Mortimers, after whom this walk has been named. It was from this family that Edward IV was descended but the most famous member of the family undoubtedly was Roger. Originally lords of nearby Wigmore Castle, the Mortimers acquired Ludlow when Roger married the heiress to the castle, Joan. Roger was one of a number of barons who opposed the weak rule of Edward II. Eventually, he was also to become the lover of Edward's wife, Isabella. Together Roger and Isabella deposed Edward and imprisoned him in Berkeley Castle where he was horribly murdered, presumably at the instigation of Roger.

Roger and Isabella set up her young son, Edward, on the throne as Edward III and thought to rule the country through him. But young sons have a tendency to grow up and Edward III avenged his father's death in 1330 when he had "proud Mortimer" executed at Tyburn in London.

8. Just over a mile after entering the Country Park the Mortimer Trail path has a hairpin bend to the right. At this point, there is a bridleway through a metal gate to the left. Leave the Mortimer Trail and follow the bridleway walking towards the north-east. Walk straight past a solitary house, Starvecrow, and, where several footpaths meet, walk straight on; there is a sign indicating Ludlow. The footpath enters a field with an old drystone wall to the left, crosses a stile and enters a small lane, finally reaching Overton Road.

9. On reaching Overton Road turn left towards Ludlow and then cross the road to walk up Lower Barns Road on the right. At the end of this cul de sac there is a gate with a sign saying "Private Property, no public right of way". This refers to the road leading directly ahead. However, a footpath that is a public right of way leads over the gate and along the left-hand side of the field, eventually crossing a stile just beside the cemetery for the little hamlet of Ludford. Walk along the road beyond and turn right to cross over the Ludford Bridge and re-enter Ludlow by walking up Lower Broad Street.

    At the top of Lower Broad Street sits the Wheatsheaf Inn, home to a rather mischievous ghost. Ladies entering this pub should beware, because the ghost here has a tendency to pinch the bottoms of ladies in the pub in order to cause trouble when these ladies then blame nearby (innocent) men. At least that is the excuse the men give! The ghost can also sometimes be heard walking around upstairs.

    Some people say that he may be an officer from the castle entering the pub through a secret passage that links the two. A little bit unlikely, but the cellars of the pub sit astride the town's old moat and subsidence in the past caused by the moat might be what gave rise to the legend of the tunnel. All the best legends have a grain of truth in them somewhere.

10. After passing the Wheatsheaf walk though the narrow Broad Gate, and to the top of Broad Street, passing the former Angel Hotel (now private apartments) where Lord Nelson stayed with both Lady Hamilton (his mistress) and her husband! A most unusual arrangement.

11. At the top of Broad Street turn right into King Street and walk along it to the Tolsey at the end of the street. From here, you cross over the Bull Ring to return to the car park.

The Tolsey is so-called because it was once a toll house where all the tolls were collected from people entering the market with their goods to trade. It was also used as a courthouse – a court of "pied poudre" or dusty feet. In other words it was a court where small complaints between local people could be dealt with rapidly, as soon as they came to town, before they had even had time to get the dust of the journey off their feet.